System Failure

A First Hand Account From The Trenches Of A Revolving Door School District

Fröderick Frankensteen

System Failure

DEDICATION

To all of those teachers who do not give into administrative pressures of nonsensical policies.

For Burch Drake: Korean War Vet, Coach, Teacher, Husband, and Artist.

For Dolin, Medrano, Winzenread, Grampa, Robinson, Coates, Coates, Collinsworth, Ohmit, Snyder, Moreno, Cheney, Mittag, Lasche, Stewart, Gahring, Mason, Benge (tact), Rojas (or Pedragon or Hart or whatever it is now), ROM, Kimes, and even, "There's a wall out there—go sit on it," Chunk.

CONTENTS

System Failure

ACKNOWLEDGMENTS

Thanks once again to the author of E8 and Hyena Falls— Tom Hite—for his editing prowess, and to yahvehjp.tumblr.com for helping to bring the cast of characters to life.

A very special thanks to all of you revolving door administrators who will go from one school to the next every two to three years and accomplish nothing (with the exception of taking a school district backwards and siphoning off money from the districts that for some reason hire you) during your administrative career, and yet will receive a better retirement package than those teachers who spent thirty-plus years in one district and actually made a difference in the lives of their students. It is because of your inability to shift the paradigm or be progressive that I pen this book to not only bring light of your ignorance to those not privy of having to deal with you on a daily basis, but to hopefully help rid the educational system of your pariah-like presence.

"*But knowledge is preferable to ignorance. Better by far to embrace the hard truth than a reassuring fable.*" – Carl Sagan

Preface

Full disclosure: this is technically a sequel. Although I would recommend reading my previous book first, not having done so will not hinder you from understanding anything that has been written here; think more "American Horror Story" than "Game of Thrones" (although both are pretty apt descriptions of the current education system). For continuity's sake, you should know that there will be some references to my previous book *The Need For Common Core* (spoiler alert: that need is dubious and deserves more study in terms of implementation than most people are giving it), and the basic cast of characters is returning with the addition of a couple of new ones.

But just in case you didn't read the previous book—or even if you did—let me (re)introduce you to the main character: RAD (twitter: @RAD_is_awesome).

RAD, if you recall, is an anagram of an acronym for Revolving Door Administrator. Yes, it's an overly convoluted and unnecessary addition to the already overburdened educational system; but then again, so is RAD.

It's important to understand that even though all RADs are administrators, not all administrators are RADs. The latter, however, are all but gone in this day and age of the revolving-door school district. These are districts with school boards that merely bring in people who parrot their ideologies, sending away the disillusioned minority of those who are actually attempting to effect positive change instead of building a résumé by which they can schlep off after two or three years of pointing fingers and counting the number of objectives and standards posted on various whiteboards. And despite recent efforts to end social promotion, close achievement gaps, and align curricula... it just seems like more and more revolving doors are being spun in tandem across the country.

Another thing to note is that the phrase *revolving-door school district* does not just refer to administration, but they are the ones who make the decisions that most affect everyone in a district; so their rotation is the most detrimental to students, teachers, parents, and everyone else in between. It also refers to some students leaving and other enrolling or, in some cases, the same student leaving and then coming back because the school that they transferred to wasn't willing to put up with their antics and gave them the boot. A revolving door school district never says *no* to a student (as each one represents thousands of dollars in funding per year) regardless as to why they were expelled from the school from whence they came. These reasons could easily be, but not limited to, using and selling drugs, getting into fights, being confrontational with teachers, as well as a number of other factors. But those reasons do not matter simply because revolving-door school districts are so desperate for money that they will take anyone who comes knocking.

A revolving door school district is also one that has an above average teacher turnover rate. Oftentimes teachers, especially those new to the profession, will land a job at one of these types of districts and come to the conclusion very rapidly that either they are not meant to be in the teaching profession, or simply that there has to be something better elsewhere. One other option is simply (if they are first or second year probationary) that they are pink-slipped—regardless of efficacy—at the end of the year as site administration for one reason or another simply does not want them to return to the district. And since these new teachers do not have tenure, then there is no due process that is necessary to let them go.

———

Whether or not you read my previous book, you might think that the acronym RAD was just something that I threw together. The reality is that it didn't dawn on me until the very end of writing the book. Originally I had tried to use letters of administrators from school years past, but couldn't come up with anything that worked. So even though RAD seems like it was an *off-the-cuff let me just put something together for the sake of writing a book*, it was actually one of the last elements to be changed from the original acronym of ALARM—where each letter was part of the name of a previous Nouveau Administrator that I had the luxury of working with for, thankfully, a very short amount of time. And even though their stay at the school site was the standard issue two-to-three years, they (there were more than five and they were all given administrative positions) were still able to do enough damage to not only my site, but other schools in the district (along with the district office) to leave it in the same state of disarray—or in most cases worse—than before they arrived. But ALARM didn't seem to flow with the content and RAD just seemed to work better because it is a reflection of what they [they being your typical revolving door administrator] think of themselves both as an administrator and their selective memory when it comes to their performance as a teacher in the classroom.

—

As you read through this book (or read the previous one) you might be wondering how I manage to find a quote from a person of interest, movie, television show, or video game to go along with a particular situation that I am writing about. For some strange reason certain quotes just seem to stick with me; though I do have to look them up in order to make sure that I get the syntax correct, I always know where it is that I need to look to find that one quote that matches the situation of which I am writing.

"This is my gift; my curse." – Peter Parker (Spiderman, 2002)

The way I look, everyone has a talent for something. Michael Jordan could slam dunk a basketball from the free-throw line, Jack Nicklaus won eighteen majors, Magnus Carlsen can play chess like few others ever could (by that I mean humans), and Thomas Edison accumulated 2,332 patents in his lifetime. As for me, well, I can take a quote from a movie, television show, or video game and use it to make a connection in the classroom or in casual conversation. Not exactly as lucrative as those just mentioned, but it does help make that which I have been writing a little bit more interesting... at least I'd like to think so.

Some of you might be thinking: *how does he get quotes from a video game?* Well, if you are someone that never delved into the realm of video games (or just haven't played them in a few decades), then you might not be aware as to how far they have come since the days of Pong. In case you are wondering, just go to YouTube and search for the end credits of Halo 4, Dishonored, or Far Cry 4 to see the magnitude of people involved in making a game today. The credits for most games roll for as long as many movies.

———

In case you haven't read my previous book, please don't let the title of that book discourage you from reading it, especially if you are an anti Common Core person; please read it from the perspective of accountability. I know it [Common Core] isn't perfect and I am the first to admit that it needs quite a few modifications (not to mention that it could stand to be a little more transparent), but without it, schools will be able to set their own parameters for what students need in order to graduate. And if you thought there was already a slight discrepancy between student learning and graduation rates, just wait, it will get worse.

But now back to RAD. Regardless as to whether or not you are in the field of education, RAD exists across all manner of domains from both the private and public sectors. So chances are you have probably had your own run-in with RAD at some point in your life irrespective of your field. Unless you are RAD and you have no idea what I am talking about which means that this book is probably not for you. Then again, no RAD ever knows that they are one, so even if you are a Nouveau Revolving Door Administrator (and I just realized I could have used DARN, but I still prefer RAD) you will probably keep reading because you wouldn't know that you are one to begin with.

"Listen, here's the thing. If you can't spot the sucker in your first half hour at the table, then you are the sucker." – Mike

(Rounders, 1998)

When it comes to education, RAD is that smug Nouveau Administrator that suddenly knows more about every subject matter—as well as how to teach them—than those of us teaching the subjects for, in some cases, decades. And although he or she has for the most part only taught at one level such as high school, middle school, or elementary school (or in the case of Coach's Story a few years of PE), they suddenly know everything there is to know about every level education. This is because they sat through some classes and wrote a few papers which led to an administrative credential as well as a "master's" degree in education which, at least in this part of the world, is all but worthless when it comes to running a school site or district. But from the perspective of money, it will push the person who received the so called "master's" degree in education a column or two over—possibly all the way to the last column—in the salary schedule thereby allowing said person to make the six-figure salary they all so deserve (sarcasm clearly intended there by the way).

One of the best parts about RAD, and believe me when I say there are many more, and the one characteristic that I really enjoy, is that they will redirect a conversation when it goes towards something they know little or almost nothing about (which is almost any and all conversations). This is usually followed by some witty response such as, "That's a little beyond my pay scale," or "I'll have to get back to you on that," which, as you probably know, they very rarely do. They will never admit that they simply don't know.

I honestly can't tell you how many emails that I have sent to administration in regards to a specific situation over the years that they have yet to get back to me on. Some administrators have openly admitted that they do not read some emails when they first see them because of the amount of words (in my case and that of another colleague, that amount of writing would be somewhere in between 500 and 1000 words at times) they contain.

So the next time an administrator asks you if, "[Y]our projector is district approved," or you receive a "reminder" email when no first instance of an email was sent out (they love gaslighting by the way, although the majority of them wouldn't know what that is), then chances are pretty high that you are dealing with RAD.

—

I'll try to stay away from (but probably won't) talking about the acts of manipulation used to keep graduation rates at an all time high as I discussed in the previous book, but I will be referencing them here and there as it is one of the more important metrics (when I say important, I mean that it is one of the parameters looked at the most when it comes to judging a school's "success" as opposed to, well, actual learning) by which schools are graded. So I will apologize upfront that there will be some overlap regarding what was written then and what has been written here.

If you would like some more entertainment on the topic of graduation rates and other nonsensical methodologies utilized by districts to maintain their image, then please visit YouTube and check out the channel *Decaying Education.*

There will more than likely be some overlap from my previous book when it comes to how much, or little, is needed for a person in education to become an administrator. But this part really needs to be stressed because they are the ones that eventually have the final say when it comes to some internet-found faux panacea that they want to force everyone to implement regardless of necessity.

Let me also add that when I speak of schools and districts using tactics to manipulate some piece of data to make it look like all is well in the eyes of the surrounding community, I am not talking about every school and district extant. I am writing about a specific type of school which is usually a lower performing, inner-city (not always but the majority of the time) school with a standard two-year revolving door for administrators. These are the schools that are slaves to short-term pedagogical fads that administrators treat as a cure for all that ails. Whether or not these fads are effective really doesn't matter to them as they [RADs] will be gone long before whatever trend they brought to the school—as well as paying a pretty penny to do so—will be shown as ineffective.

In other words, I am not talking about a school that is on their third principal in the last fifty years—yes, you read that correctly. Believe it or not, those types of schools with a strong foundation do still exist. These are the schools that perform on every level be it academics, athletics, or any other activity that the school may partake of.

The schools that I am speaking of are those similar to that of the one I have worked at for a near twenty years. If you don't count the interim principals, then I have seen at least ten different principals in less than twenty years of service. In the same amount of time, the district itself has seen at least seven different people sitting at the helm in the office of the superintendent. In addition to that, with the board actions that have taken place about a third of the way through 2018, I will have also worked with eight different vice principals in a span of four years. There you go local board of education—decisions like those are the ones that give a low performing, inner-city school the solidarity that they so badly need (sarcasm once again, intended).

What really made this year interesting is that neither of the two new vice principals have any administrative experience when it comes to the high school level. In fact, one of them has no administrative experience at all and their entire teaching career was at an elementary school. The second vice principal is on a third assignment in the last four years (and has already been reassigned to another site for the 2018–2019 school year; which makes it the fourth site in five years). I can already sense the eye-rolling that those of you reading this are doing as you have probably been through a similar experience.

I originally did not pass judgment as it was completely possible that these people would end up doing a good job. But as history repeated itself again, both of the newbie administrators (although the one who was already transferred did so to a much greater degree) would treat the high school students in the same fashion as those of their elementary counterparts. And just for emphasis, one of the two was reassigned earlier in the year to a cushy cubicle in the back of the district office for the 2018–2019 school year.

"But time flows like a river and history repeats." – The Secret of Mana, 1993

With this type of revolving door administration, how will it ever be possible for these low performing schools to build, maintain, and add to an educational infrastructure when every couple of years a new set of people with "new" ideas take over? They will more than likely throw out that which was implemented over the last two years, and then start the entire process anew by putting their own policies into action—which will be the same as those that were just thrown out but with a different acronym—without first doing some due diligence to see if said policies are even necessary. These types of schools far outnumber those that, as I previously mentioned, have had three principals in a fifty-year time span. These types of low performing schools will simply continue along their current route (and joined by others) as long as the system continues down the same path without realizing that it's lost in the Tulgey Wood looking for a Cheshire cat for guidance.

———

I will try to keep things pretty generic so anyone in the teaching profession (or just a person on the outside looking in) anywhere regardless of the subject can identify with the issues that we are facing in the educational system as it stands at the moment.

As I mentioned a few paragraphs ago, this is the year 2018 so I should probably create a little context for you just in case you are reading this in the year 2037. Maybe by then the school that I will have retired from (assuming I stay there until then or it closes due to the rapid declining enrollment) will actually be offering its second computer programming class.

There currently is not much in the way of accountability when it comes to the curriculum that any particular school has to offer. The California High School Exit Exam (CAHSEE) was discarded; which made a number of admin happy (though they will never admit it) as there were too many students who could not pass the eighth-grade (at best) math portion of the test. Although there was a little more success with the tenth-grade language arts section of the CAHSEE, it was still too much of an obstacle for many students to overcome; not to mention that it was hurting some schools' near perfect graduation rate. It was also an exam that an academically strong fifth-grade student could have passed; I'm not saying they would have aced the test, but definitely could have passed it.

The Common Core exams are still in the early stages of development. Students are taking these exams at the end of the year, but there really is no definitiveness as to the meaning of the results, nor does there seem to be any hurry to figure out what the scores are telling us.

And if you are reading this in the year 2037, then you probably know the outcome of the whole issue with Common Core, and whether or not receiving a high school diploma ever became dependent on the outcome of how a student performed on the exams (if that did happen, then graduation rates would have plummeted). The AP tests are probably still around and schools are more than likely offering as many of these classes as they can in order to attract students to their school, but not really advertising the results.

In other words, we are currently in a phase of educational limbo. With so much confusion over Common Core (much of which can be attributed to both district and site administration), it is unlikely that we will be leaving this pedagogical purgatory anytime soon. Many schools are enjoying this phase as there is no real sense of urgency when it comes to trying to improve upon the previous year. What they are enjoying (at least in California) is a nice little increase in the graduation rate since the CAHSEE is now defunct.

Finally, as was the case in my previous book, the majority of the situations will be taken from the perspective of a high school math teacher. Although I am familiar with what goes on before and after high school when it comes to academia, this is the level that most people seem to pay attention to when it comes to the lack of preparation for college, or just life for that matter, which takes places from grade nine to grade twelve.

- 1 -

Regressive Education

Despite what you may have heard, the problem with America's education system is not that it's broke... but that it's broken. Funding is an issue, of course, and the equitable distribution of monies needs to be more closely monitored and examined in such a way that it will truly support students across the country is a worthy and important focus. But there are some things that are in dire need of being repaired that aren't found in any bookkeeping ledger, unless what they're keeping track of is the upside-down pyramid that is the system of accountability and administration.

It's not exactly a secret that the system is broken and it seems that many districts have a similar approach in attempting to fix their own internal problems. The most common solution (though not so much of a solution as it is giving jobs to friends) is for the local school board to put people who they know and agree with in terms of educational ideologies into the top positions over at the district office. Those top people then bring in their friends (through a sham interview process) to run the local school sites to help fix generations of problems (referred to as "changing the culture") in a mere two-to-three years.

If you have been around long enough, then you are fully aware that this type of cronyism not only does not help the schools, students, and surrounding communities, but also only results in exacerbating the problems of already dysfunctional school districts.

So then why not just identify low performing districts, fire everyone, and start from scratch? Although an entire reset of a district is a possibility, it is very rare with the exception of the state coming in and taking over—which really means that the school district has some serious problems (usually financial) when that does happen... but an upper management shuffle normally occurs annually, especially in lower performing, inner-city school districts. This rearrangement of site administration will usually take place during a June or July board meeting when no one is paying attention. This is also the time that boards will vote on a number of items that were tabled during the school year and pass them as no one will be around to cause a kerfuffle.

But if you have worked for a school district, or simply dealt with one long enough, then you have probably seen very few, if any, actual changes regarding the fundamental purpose of what is supposed to be happening within the walls of each school that resides in the district.

The main dilemma (one of many but you will soon see that those many stem from the one) with education today is that RAD is in charge of making the decisions for an entire school district or particular site depending on their *given* position. As I talked about in my previous book, the superintendent will bring in his or her handpicked support staff that will, for the most part, see eye-to-eye with his or her decisions. Many of them often started ascending the ladder of administration after a few years of classroom experience, and that which they do have is often at a mismatched level (a former elementary teacher being appointed as a high school administrator, for example).

Like anything, there are exceptions to this issue, but the majority of Nouveau Administration usually falls within the guise of what was just mentioned. But it is also not a surprise to anyone that the revolving door of administration has been detrimental to most of the schools across America.

———

Let's first get into the nuances of education in the classroom today. One issue (along with countless others) is that education has morphed very little when it comes to what is being taught in today's schools. Many schools are still teaching, for the most part, the same subjects today (the year 2018) as they were in the '90s, '80s, or even '70s; which isn't necessarily a bad thing and, believe it or not, is really the least of the worries. The issue is that very little has been added (though many things have been subtracted) to enrich the educational experience, as well as to add to the core curriculum classes that are a reflection of world around us.

Not only has it changed very little in regards to pedagogical practices, but many schools have regressed when it comes to the variety of course offerings in their schedule of classes. In other words, we are actually teaching less when it comes to the number of topics than we used to in an era when we could, and should, be teaching much more.

The main argument that you will hear, or give, in regards to the previous paragraphs is that it is not the same as decades earlier because there is obviously more technology—which I will focus on in the chapter *The 21st Century Classroom*—being used in the classroom to assist the students with the learning process. There is plenty of evidence that this is true and schools across the country now have multiple computer labs and are also assigning students their own electronic devices, such as a tablet or laptop.

The problem is the assumption that all of this technology and access to information is somehow going to automatically do more to assist with the learning process. The reality is, however, that this abundance of tech is doing more to hinder the process of teaching and learning, as well as creating an environment where students expect to find answers by typing or speaking questions into their phone.

"Today it's much different. Information swarms us, comforts us, it disrupts us. It's an age of infinite distraction, for those so willing." – Dr. Michael Burry (UCLA Economics Commencement, 2012)

And yet, if you were to simply reminisce back over your many years of schooling (especially those of you who have been removed from the classroom for a good ten years or so) you will find that not much has changed in the majority of school districts across the country. In fact, if you were to visit any of your childhood educational stomping grounds, aside from some upgrades in technology and possibly some new desks, new carpeting, and maybe even a paint job here or there, what really goes on within the walls of the school with regards to education has only not improved, but is realistically going in the wrong direction.

Not only is there a decline in the variety of course options when it comes to the available curriculum, but the quality of education is also headed in the same direction. Administration—mainly those at the district office that make the decisions for each site to follow—are so concerned and enamored with standardized testing and collecting data (although their understanding of what that data is telling them or how to interpret the data is mediocre at best) that many classes are simply being removed from a school's master schedule to focus on those classes that will result in better test scores; thereby validating the district office adjustments and allowing them to gloat about the changes that were made and how they resulted in higher test scores.

Then, of course, they'll brag about these scores (because at least one of the myriad of measurements will show an increase in something good, or a decrease in something bad) and use them as evidence as to how the school district is better preparing each student for their eventual collegiate and real-world experiences. And for the majority of instances, these administrators that do the bragging about how schools are preparing their students for college are inadvertently telling the truth. The reason that many students' initial college experience will closely resemble that of high school is because many of them will end up in remedial classes once they start their post-secondary education. These classes will essentially be equivalent to those they took in high school with the exception that this time they are paying for books and tuition—usually through borrowed money.

Now if the results are not an improvement, or even go the wrong direction, then the solution will be the same reaction (which they will refer to as being *proactive*) as it always has been: spend more money (which will usually take place in the form of trainings, expensive software, electronic devices, and more conferences for administrators). Administration will then sign the teachers up for multiple trainings (the cost of which will easily be in the tens of thousands of dollars) over the next twelve months in order to increase the lackluster test scores that the school just received. One colleague missed almost twenty percent of instructional days during the 2016–2017 school year because of the number of trainings she was "volunteered" to attend.

This is very standard practice from district office officials as the solution to poor test scores. Take teachers out of the classroom and leave the students with a substitute. And this action of pulling teachers out of the classroom will somehow increase student learning and performance on standardized testing. So if decisions like these are coming down from the district office, then shouldn't site administration be included and agree with the actions of the district? Well, yes, yes they should. And since we are talking about RAD (do you really think that they are suddenly going to grow a spine?), they will not only agree with whatever the decision might be, but will also praise the decisions and those making it as paradigm-shifting or progressive or proactive or some other eduspeak adjective.

—

Since I'm on the subject, there are plenty of people that are against standardized testing and feel that students shouldn't be taking these exams (whether they be AP, SAT, Common Core or just chapter tests out of a book) as they do nothing to prepare students for the real world. There are those who argue that students should not be graded on how well they do on tests or homework at all, but rather on that of their potential as to how well they *could* have done as opposed to how well they actually did (I'm not even going to go down that path).

"Test people. It's a way to find out what you know. But don't then say if you don't know this, therefore the rest of your life is screwed!" – Neil deGrasse Tyson (Interview with Bill Moyers)

I have had arguments with those I work with, be they administration or teachers, that want to limit the number of exams (be they standardized or just a unit exam for a class) a student takes in a year, or just eliminate them altogether. Some argue that final exams are useless because they offer nothing in regards to preparing students for their future. For those of you who think that, maybe you should consider paying attention to your everyday happenings—as life is really just one exam after another.

I know people who will argue that a bad test score could lead to a low grade which could then lead to low self-esteem, and might also hurt a student's chances of getting into the college of their choice once they graduate from high school. I have worked with people that do limit the number of exams or give practice exams that turn out to be the actual exam so that all the students who take it receive a good grade. And if they don't, well they just keep taking it again and again until they get the "A" that they think is deserved.

I will take the other side of the argument and say that testing (be it standardized or not) does prepare students for a post K–12 environment whether that be attending college, going out and getting a job, or even starting your own business. You want to be a lawyer? You need to pass the Bar exam. You want to be a mechanic? You need to pass the Automotive Service Excellence (ASE) exam. You want to be a doctor? Then you are going to have to pass multiple exams. Want to work for Google? You are going to be tested and graded. What about Microsoft? You are going to be tested and graded. Want to have your own talk show? Your test is your performance every time you take the stage and your grade will be your ratings. And if those ratings are not good enough, then there is a high likelihood that the show will be canceled. In other words, you got a bad grade on your test and, in this case, you are out of a job.

In fact, just the interview process to get any job is essentially a test by which you are being graded. If you fail, then you do not get the job (unless you are friends with the superintendent of a school district, which means you will get the job regardless of your abilities). And it is this type of failure that students are simply not prepared for once they leave the K–12 school system because the system never gave them the opportunity to learn from that which they failed.

"There are no secrets to success. It is the result of preparation, hard work, and learning from failure." – Colin Powell

Some students will then argue that they won't need to get a job (and many students have when I bring up the subject of being graded in this manner) because they will eventually start their own business, thus allowing them to be their own boss and not have to answer to anyone. I usually respond in the following manner: If you do have your own company and are publicly traded (which usually leads to a lesson as to how the stock market works), then you will have shareholders that not only grade you, but can actually sue you if the share price goes in the wrong direction. And if you are a publicly traded company, then shareholders can have you fired in a similar manner to that of Steve Jobs in the early days of Apple.

Not a public company? Well, you will still need to come up with something that your customers will buy and continue to innovate to keep them interested in using whatever the product is that you are producing. And if interest somehow wanes in whatever your company does produce, then the company goes under and your F is way worse than any F you will have received on a test in school.

The point is, we are all tested and graded on a daily basis from that of our job to the way we dress. Someone is always grading us in one way, shape, or form. Some grades don't have much of an affect—if any at all—on us as a person. I probably get an F for the way I dress on a daily basis, but that doesn't have any impact on my life whatsoever. But if I'm late with a proposal or don't meet a deadline that has been set for months, then receiving an F for not being prepared could be detrimental to my very being.

So do these standardized tests (or just regular chapter exams or homework) that we give students every year help them to better prepare for those that I just mentioned? Maybe not explicitly for all of the previously mentioned, but it does give them a heads-up on what will eventually happen. Is it perfect? Not by any means. Is there room for improvement? There is, and always will be. But for all of those who oppose it and say that it does nothing to prepare students for a life beyond school, well you might be one of those rare people who are never tested, but as for the rest of us, life is really one test after another on just about a daily basis.

—

Standardized testing is one reason that many schools are reducing their class offerings. This leads to a school whose schedule of class offerings is more focused on doing well on these exams as opposed to actual learning. But the reaction of schools converging on a smaller number of specific classes to focus on the testing (thereby keeping the spotlight on what is taught in the classroom on a specific number of standards) so that the scores will increase which, in turn, will make the school look better isn't—as many people would like to think—the fault of the tests themselves.

The fault, not surprisingly, is with administration's misinterpretation that certain standards put forth by the College Board (AP), Common Core, or whatever else comes up in the future for that matter, are the only things that should be explicitly taught in the classroom. And it is this reaction by district and site administration that has caused so many schools to narrow their vision on what should be offered, and also what has caused this educational inertia that we have been experiencing for at least the last two decades.

I'll get back to this topic of standardized testing, as well as that which it begat in the form of standardized learning (if that is even possible) a few chapters from now.

Another part of the problem that is keeping us in this state of stagnation (at best) is that for some unfathomable reason, the only option after high school (regardless of preparation) is to go straight to college. It's as if a student's entire K–12 experience is to build to this crescendo that sends them off to at least four more years of schooling (four years being a very unlikely reality as six seems to be a little more realistic, *if* they actually finish). It's this early indoctrination into the K–12 system that leads students to believe that the only option in life is to finish high school, go off to college, then get a job that best suits whatever degree they spend a minimum of four years earning and, as it is for most students, attaining tens of thousands of dollars in student loan debt.

I'm not really exactly sure when it began, but the push for more and more students to go to college with the emphasis being to attend a four-year university straight out of high school is rapidly becoming the only option presented to students. This insistence begins at a very early age that leads them to believe that going to college is the only way to succeed in life. Granted, there is nothing wrong with already explaining the future options (notice I used the plural there as they should be taught that life offers more choices than just going to college) that students will have at an early age; but to insist that taking classes from age five (or earlier) until the early to mid-to-late twenties is the only path available is somewhat Orwellian or Kafkaesque.

The idea that the only path to success (success usually being defined as a higher standard of living vis-à-vis a big house and a nice car) is through college and only through college takes away the individualistic thought of straying from a preset path to see if there are any other trails that are less often explored or, better yet, to create one's own (I was going to say *blaze* one's own trail, but that has a completely different meaning— especially in high school). And speaking from experience, if you are a teacher and do try to tell your students that college is not the only option, then you better be ready for a meeting with an administrator or, at the very least, an indignant email that explains that our job as teachers is to educate and going to college is how the educational process is completed.

Therein represents one of the major problems of the push for going straight to college. Starting from the early years, college is sold to students as the means by which success is achieved. Now there are plenty of arguments both for and against that, but that's obviously not the point I'm trying to get at here.

As a side note to the *everyone-goes-to-college* movement: the last few years there have been more students asking for make-up work from previous years because they have a grade on their transcript that might keep them from getting into the four-year school of their choice. Now I can't speak for any other schools outside of my own district in regards to this as I have not heard anything (yet) from any neighboring schools, or friends who work at schools in other counties or states, but this request from students for make-up work from a year or two previous will more than likely be coming to your school very soon.

In short, some counselors and administrators are having students with a D (just as an example) on their transcript for a core class that might keep them from getting into a university, request work so that they can have the grade changed. So a student will go to a teacher from a previous year and ask for work in order to raise a grade on their transcript. The request itself is always just for a chapter or two of work but never for any sort of assessment. Teachers are even getting visits from counselors and administrators in the hopes of coercing them into giving some work to the student to raise a grade; usually from the student's sophomore or junior year.

One colleague in the social science department had one of these-such visits from the vice principal in charge of curriculum regarding a student who *earned* a D his junior year. After enough persuasion from the standard two-year administrator, the teacher agreed to give the student two weeks to do three assignments. These assignments were not easy and each would have required tens of hours of work on the part of the student.

The two weeks passed and the student returned to the teacher with one of the three assignments (no, it wasn't complete), and a grade-change form. The student honestly felt that the teacher was going to change the grade based on one-third of the agreed upon work. When the teacher inquired as to the whereabouts of the other two tasks, the student simply responded that he was too busy with senior activities to complete the other two assignments. In other words, even after a second chance a year later, the student felt that completing 33% of the required work would be enough to merit a change of grade to get into whatever university that he had applied to. The teacher didn't change the grade, even after another visit from the administrator for one last request with graduation a mere couple of days away.

So for those of you teaching high school and have never heard of this yet, be patient; this action of requesting work from previous years to raise a grade to get into a four-year school is coming to a campus near you (and yours as well).

"Like the man in the stall said to the man waiting: give me time baby." – Al Bundy (Married With Children)

—

From a very early age, students are shown graphs of how much money a person with a college degree will earn over their lifetime in comparison to that of a person with just a high school diploma or no diploma at all. We've all seen these graphs growing up and still see them in articles and posted up around campus about how a college degree pays off in the long run. And just in case you forgot what one looks like, here you go.

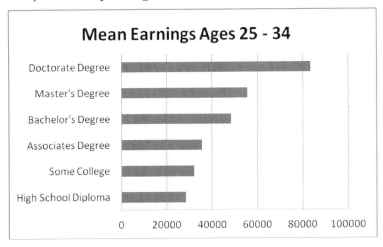

Source: US Census Bureau 2008

For starters, not everyone attributes success to how much money is in their bank account or what kind of car they drive. These just seem to be the metrics that are often used by many in society to judge a person's worth. Secondly, showing just a mean or median really does not do much to explain what is really going on behind the numbers, but the mean is usually the number that is shown when it comes to graphs like the one posted. Sadly, most people (especially administrators) do not understand statistical analysis and usually end up showing the teaching staff, or students, graphs like the one you just saw in order to try and validate their point.

"Gentlemen, we got 20 calls about the David Hyde-Pierce incident. And as you know, one call equals a billion people; which means 20 billion people were offended by this." – FCC Suit (Family Guy)

One aspect that is missing is time needed to earn each degree shown—not to mention the opportunity costs of staying in school until your mid-to-late twenties. It is very unlikely (regardless of the field of study) that a student will earn a PhD before the age of twenty-five... but if you did, and it's not in the field of education (as some universities are starting to offer a PhD in education... online), then congratulations—there may be no conceivable way to measure the sheer act of human will that accomplishing such a feat requires. There's not a chart for measuring human will... but if there were, then we can be assured that RAD would create a pacing guide for it and a benchmark as a means of assessing it.

Another missing component (which might be considered slightly important to a future college graduate, and even more important to those who start and do not finish their post-secondary education) that many schools do not talk about is the price of earning each one of those degrees. And as you more than likely know, the cost of each one of those degrees has gone up dramatically since 2008. The fact that this discussion of debt rarely, if ever, comes up in a high school classroom, or in a conversation between a future college student and a counselor or administrator, is appalling to say the least. Perhaps the graph should also include the average amount of debt incurred at each level and the average amount of years it takes to pay off those loans. Maybe there's hope for developing that human-will chart after all.

The thing about this push for college is that all of us know people who are doing quite well that do not have a four-year college degree. Some of these people are even doing better financially, in some cases much better, than those of us that did traverse the path of the university. Many of these people are not saddled with huge amounts of student loan debt because they did not attend an expensive college; though some did attend a tech or trade school, they did not have to pay what are rapidly becoming exorbitant (no, that is not hyperbole) tuition fees that colleges and universities are charging.

I know people in the construction industry, mechanics, painters, plumbers, photographers, and other areas that are doing very well and, in many cases, better than those of us that spent a good four years (at least) to earn that degree. It is important to note that I don't just mean "better" in the sense of making more money. These people that I know who did not get their college degree are just as articulate, well-read, great communicators, have great critical thinking skills and, well, the list goes on in comparison to the people (many of which are administrators) who I know that have received at least one college degree.

No, it didn't happen immediately, and many of them did, as I mentioned, attend a trade school to learn their craft or, in the case of a painter, has simply done it for so long that he has a name and reputation for himself in the company that employs him. In some instances, if a commercial property calls the company he works for, they will not offer the contract to the company unless this specific person is on the job. The one fact to point out and stress with all of those examples is that their success did not happen overnight; it took years for them to get to where they are at today.

———

This underlying expectation of immediate success in an age of instant feedback through Twitter, Facebook, Instagram, or other forms of social media, or simply finding the answers to a question—where the typing of the question takes longer than finding the answer—is something that many students are accustomed to from a young age and are not familiar with the process of life; that it is more often than not, much slower than getting a heart on a tweet.

The whole idea that success is immediate is disrupting both the teaching and learning processes. The funny thing is that it really doesn't start that way. Something happens along the educational timeline where students go from discovering on their own with teachers and parents as guides along the way, to just being told how to do something in order to find an answer in return for a grade. This process of education where answers are found by typing something into a search-bar, or speaking into a phone, is taking away from the discovery that most of us were brought up on. One thing that is comical about this *cognita novum* is how many administrators who are observing a class will consider looking up an answer on an electronic device—then regurgitating it for the teacher—as evidence of learning instead of the rote production of duplicate information that it ultimately represents.

One administrator gave a similar example as to what they considered to be a "good" teacher during an observation. The teacher would ask their students a question, give them some time to look up the answer, and then give a reward (as stipulated by the PBIS guidelines) to the students that came up with the right answer in the shortest amount of time. Yes, this is what many administrators—namely RAD—consider to be teaching and learning in a 21st century classroom. If you are a psychiatrist or animal trainer, you might recognize these positive feedback techniques. And if you are a teacher, don't you dare forget about giving out the PBIS rewards to a student for typing a question into an electronic device and writing down what it was they found. Who's a good teacher? That's right, *you're* a good teacher. And so was RAD—so good that they can train you the same way they trained their students.

Education is a hierarchy-based business now, and in lieu of actually demonstrating pedagogical excellence (which is admittedly very difficult to measure or even define), those with the highest degree get to be at the top of the food-chain, or the pay-grade as it is known by those who equate value with net-worth, are also the ones who evaluate teachers and ultimately decide (based on the evaluation process) which teachers are good, and which are bad.

This process of rating which teachers are effective and which ones are ineffective is reserved only for those in the administrative domain. These are the people who—because they are in possession of the correct paperwork—will evaluate teachers at a school they have never taught at, and as so often happens, for a subject they have never taught. So even though they will be gone after a couple of years, the evaluation that they gave to a teacher that they barely knew will stay with that teacher until he or she retires.

———

Some teachers are starting to simply give-in when it comes to trying to get students to think and problem solve. The reason for this is simple: If a student can't solve a problem, then they might not get a good grade; and if they don't get a good grade, then it might hurt their GPA; and if their GPA goes down, then they might not be able to get into the college of their choice, and most importantly, if a student fails some classes, then they might not be able to graduate—which would hurt the school's near perfect graduation rate along with the student's self-esteem. And if any of these things do happen, then a teacher will more than likely will find themselves in defense mode at a student, parent, teacher, and admin conference which, after so many of these, is just not worth the stress when the outcome of the meeting is, more often than not, in favor of the student. Not to mention that you don't want to be an immoral person for keeping a student out of college, do you?

"I think it is immoral for a teacher to ever give a grade lower than a C to a college bound student." – AP Teacher at a curriculum meeting in regards to a student who wasn't accepted to the four-year school of their choice because of a D that was earned in an AP class.

Perhaps this teacher, and others like them, should reconsider what they believe is morally correct. Is never giving a grade lower than a C to a college bound student really a moral thing to do? Is setting them up for failure by only giving students C's or higher just because they want to go straight to a four-year university after high school really moral? Is giving a student grades that aren't earned—thereby giving said student a false sense of accomplishment—really what some teachers consider to be moral? In the case of this particular teacher (and there are others), the answer would be *yes* as the teacher in question rarely failed a student.

Then again, this is the same teacher who would *miraculously* find work for a student to raise their grade to an A or B if a parent or administrator were to contact them and question why a particular student had a low mark in the class. Apparently, giving a student a grade less than a C when it is merited is immoral, but changing grades without justification just to appease a parent, counselor, or administrator for the sake of not having to attend a meeting is somehow moral. And if you have been in the classroom long enough, then it's more than likely you work with a similar person.

———

Schools and districts that fit the description I have been talking about are the ones that are experiencing a double whammy when it comes to trying to keep up with what is happening in the world around them. Not only are they removing hands-on, pragmatic classes that teach students a skill, but they are also not replacing these classes with anything that would help a student to prepare for the world in which we live. This bifurcation by the majority of schools taking this path will only increase the ever-growing educational gap between the students that graduate from a school that lowers the bar in order to keep the graduation rate up, to the ones who graduate from a school that is keeping up with education as it reflects in the world around them.

So for those school district administrators—yes, I'm talking to you, RAD— who make the decisions to offer less when it comes to a variety of classes because you let standardized testing dictate what classes you offer, while concurrently worrying that your graduation rate might drop resulting in a decrease in enrollment, hopefully you will at some point realize what so many around you already do... then again we are talking about RAD so unless it can be expressed with a chart, slogan, or acronym then it's probably just not gonna get past that human will to remain ignorant; which RAD seems to be trying to prove is as limitless as it is immeasurable.

- 2 -

Students First

We've all heard someone, somewhere, at some time, utter those words that we have become accustomed to hearing from some person (usually a site or district administrator) working for a school district. If you are a parent (especially one who is active in the education of your child or children), then you may have attended your share of meetings where you have heard these words spoken by many an admin. Regardless as to whether those are the monthly board meetings, the parent-teacher association gatherings, or perhaps one of the "Coffee with the Superintendent," or "Breakfast with the Principal" events, or with some other administrator that really wants to convey the message that your son or daughter is the most important person to them and the district.

Even if the last time you stepped onto a public school campus was when you were attending your own graduation (or when you decided that you'd had enough and just weren't going to go anymore), you have heard these words spoken to the point of ad nauseam. I can also assure you that the phrase expressed by so many will continue until our sun goes nova in order to prey on the emotions of those who will listen. And if you read this in the voice you imagine me to have, even though I'm just another "some person" in education, you can probably hear a *sigh* and sense an eye-roll as many of you have probably done yourself when the words are spoken: "The students come first."

Doesn't it feel hollow, though?

That's because it's missing half of the truth. And although I'm just "some person", I have the experience and practice to offer up the other half—the part that you may have always cynically suspected is the case, but was never explicitly told by anyone in a position to give an honest answer: "The students come first... because they are the foundational basis of funding."

Now does that mean your kid is just a walking dollar sign? Kind of... in fact, yes, on a certain unavoidable level. This is because ADA (Average Daily Attendance—you might want to remember this acronym and whenever you do read it just think one thing: money) is calculated by the number of students who attend over half of their classes per day; which is specifically tied to the amount of funds the district will receive by the state. It is an attempt to ensure equity to schools based on their needs, but like any good intention, it has paved the road to a special kind of educational hell in which accountability measures are tied to student success, and student success is tied to their classroom performance, and their classroom performance is tied to... well, that's kind of the problem.

"The speeches we heard today were nothing more than words." – George Oscar Bluth (Arrested Development... and if you suddenly hear Europe's *Final Countdown* playing in your head, I don't blame you.)

I doubt that it would surprise anyone to find out that the majority of administrators, much like any politician, will tell you whatever it is you want to hear in order to keep you [the parent or guardian] happy to keep your child (or children) enrolled in the district. After all, if the average daily attendance were to drop for some reason, then many of these administrators risk losing their six-figure paying job along with their $300—in many cases more—per month car allowance and a monthly cell phone allowance (which is something that I just found out about this year from a principal who was complaining that he was only getting fifty dollars per month for his). Then again, administrators are usually the last to get cut as teachers and support-staff are usually first on the chopping block.

If you are a teacher, then you have probably heard these words at the annual district gathering at the beginning of the school year. This is when the superintendent gets up in front of all of the employees and talks about his or her vision of where the district is headed; and how important it is that we all understand that the students come first. He or she will then give their amazing *how I changed a struggling school as a first-year principal* story, followed by why they took the giant leap into administration and how we should all work together to make this vision (which is solely the vision of the superintendent) happen. This is usually accompanied by some inspirational YouTube video to get everyone excited for the up-and-coming school year.

And if you are a teacher, then you probably also hear those words often stated so many times in a faculty meeting, or over the public announcement system from the principal, or some other administrator at the school where you are working. More than likely, you have also received an email from administration somewhere that uses the phrase in order to put emphasis on some sort of course of action that they decided on with very little input, if any at all, from teachers or parents.

Now to back track for a little, when I refer to this type of administration, you should know that I am speaking of the Nouveau Administration where the majority of individual administrators within the administration have earned the title of RAD. There are admin out there (although much fewer and farther between) that really do put students first and do believe it and, more importantly, mean it when they say it. These are also the same administrators that will not fold to the pressures from the district office because they are more worried about their job placement for next year as opposed to doing the job that they are supposed to be doing. But being that the majority of hires under the current superintendent are always brought in by the superintendent, and given high paid administrative jobs regardless of their qualifications (aside from the fact they are in possession of a specific piece of paper that allows them to hold an administrative position—though there is a workaround to the piece of paper issue which I will talk about later), they will simply do what they are told regardless of whether or not their actions really do put students first.

The superintendent that spouts off "students first" is also the same person that will tell the principal(s) at the school sites in the district that they need to lay off x amount of teachers for the next school year. This reduction of teachers is usually based on the full-time enrollment projections, and if that hypothetical number is less than the current number then the conclusion—at least from an administrative standpoint—is always the same: cut more teachers and support staff.

Granted, there are occasionally times when there are too many teachers on a staff such that if and when there is a substantial drop to the number of students at a school (such as when a new school opens down the road), then it might be necessary to let some teachers go; the first of which will be the ones at the bottom of the seniority list regardless of how effective they may be in the classroom. But this is very rarely the case as many of the cutbacks are usually based on projected numbers as opposed to the actual number of bodies that show up on the first day of school. What ends up happening is that the school enrollment is usually plus or minus a few students from where the number was from the previous year. The only difference (which really isn't a difference because this has happened every year for as far back as I can remember) is that the classes will be packed at or beyond the cap of the contractual number of students per teacher. This can be— depending on the district and grade level—anywhere from fifteen to one, or in the case of the school where I work (or worked at depending on whatever year it is that you are reading this), thirty-six to one. The physical education classes, in case you were wondering, are usually around sixty-to-seventy students per teacher... not easy.

And all the while that teachers and support staff are getting cut and class sizes are expanding, there are very rarely any cuts at the administrative level. In fact, more often than not, a new administrative position will open up and the job will usually go to someone that has known the superintendent, board members, or both, for a number of years. Or perhaps the district office secretary needs a secretary of their own because the work-load is simply too much for one person to handle. Also consider that many of these administrative positions are almost always (at least in the case of my district and surrounding districts) much higher in pay than the teacher that was released both on an absolute and hourly scale.

"Seymour the teachers are fed up. You have to start putting money back into the school. You've cut back on everything: salaries, supplies, the food... I don't care what you say, I can taste the newspaper." – Edna Krabappel (The Simpsons)

Just to give you a little idea of the numbers, the teachers that are released first will also be the newer teachers usually making the least. An administrator—depending on what level of administration—could easily be making two to five times that of a new teacher and even possibly more than five. If you go simply by gross pay, the interim superintendent of my district makes almost four times the amount of a new teacher. If you were to include other allowances and benefits, then this interim superintendent (who will more than likely have the interim part removed at a July board meeting and given a nice raise in the face of declining enrollment) is the equivalent of five first-year teachers.

The majority of high ranking district office administrators very rarely make any visits to the schools in the district. Yes, occasionally they will ingratiate a site with a visit, but any such visit is rarely a voluntary event, and has more to do with some other catalyst for the visit; such as a board member, active parent, or both, who are interested in observing all of the amazing pedagogical strategies that administration—be they district or site—are constantly bragging about. The way this usually works is that district admin will contact site admin, who will then send out an email telling teachers about the visit a few days ahead of time. Site administration will then take whomever the important persons are on a tour of classrooms around the campus and, although it will appear that the visited classrooms are randomly chosen, they, in reality, will be teachers that were hand selected by RAD and given ample warning as to not only when the visit will take place, but also what they expect to observe on the day of the visit.

As a side note, going back a couple of paragraphs, the now previous superintendent and the long-standing board president have known each other for many, many years. Not that this would shock anyone, but I thought it necessary to convey the obvious cronyism that occurs when it comes to giving the higher paying administrative jobs to those with the connections as opposed to those who are best suited for the position.

In my near twenty years in the classroom, I have seen on average a new principal about every two years, and new superintendent about every three years. I honestly could not even tell you how many vice principals that I have seen come and go during this same timeframe. And during their short time at this district, the majority (if not all) had received at least one raise during their stay. Even though each and every single one of them constantly used the phrase "students first", no one was ever fooled by those words with the exception of the board members who hired these people, and those trying to curry their favor with constant sycophantic behavior.

Granted, the previous superintendent did get a couple bond measures passed to get new carpet in the classrooms, new desks, and even an eighty inch monitor in many of the classrooms, the fact of the matter remains that sites like the picture that you are about to see are all too common throughout the majority of classrooms across the country. The stacks of books you see in the following picture are from the social science department. Now I do understand that books—especially in the public school system—do go through standard wear and tear that will eventually lead to deterioration. But to put this picture into perspective (keep in mind that this is the year 2018), the last time the social science department received new books, well, George W. Bush was just starting his second term.

Also understand that the books in the picture do not represent all of the books for that subject and that there are some books that are still in pretty good shape—even after fourteen years, but they are slowly approaching the condition of the books in the picture that follows. Every subject has books of this condition, but those in the social science are by far the worst because they haven't received any new books—with the exception of an occasional replacement—in over a decade.

Those that you see below are from a class set that the teacher would use. Many students do not bring their assigned books to class as this school does not have any lockers for students to store their things when they bring them to school. And as often as our administration talks about putting students first, and as often as they have visited classrooms with sights like these, they never seem interested in doing something about it; at least until a parent finally speaks up, then suddenly they are worried about the condition of the books, desks, outdoor lighting fixtures, or whatever a parent criticizes when it comes to the allocation of monies.

Views like this are all too common in classrooms irrespective of the state and—with very few exceptions—school districts. And regardless of who is sitting in the admin offices, they will be more than happy take their raises all the while many students and teachers have to make use of "books" that have very little, if any, binding left to hold everything together.

The first argument that can easily be made is that many books are going digital and there is no reason to pay for the adoption of new textbooks; which is a valid point. That being said, the last adoption year for the social science department would have been back in 2011 when digital copies of books were not so readily available and not everyone was walking around with a supercomputer in their pocket. But even with students using digital copies in the near future, that picture is really just an insult to not only the teachers in the classroom, but to the students and parents as well. Let's not forget to mention that it really isn't anything new and has been an ongoing problem for decades.

Most of us remember checking out books from the librarian back in high school and trying to get the good books with some binding left and pages that weren't stuck together with bubblegum... at least that's what we were hoping was sticking those pages together.

Another issue to point out is that the math and English departments are not suffering quite as much when it comes to new books. So why are other subject areas being put on the back burner when it comes to the textbook adoption cycle? Well, it's because they are not yet part of the new Common Core exams. Since these are the only two subject areas that are the focus of these exams, it makes perfect sense to those over at the district office not to allocate funds on a subject that isn't being tested. And as long as they are not part of the testing cycle, then they will be made to suffer when it comes to the monies that are made available for book funding.

The words [students first] have been said by so many

people (be they in the educational field or not) such as teachers, parents, and administration—not surprisingly the ones who use it the most—that the phrase itself seems to be nothing more than semantic satiation.

"I've said Jiminy Jillickers so many times the words have lost all meaning." – Millhouse Van Houten (The Simpsons)

The thing is that those who really do put the students first are also not the ones that go around touting "students first". These are the people involved in the educational process that go out of their way to do everything that they can for the students, as well as the surrounding community, without the desire to call attention to their actions nor the need to spread the word of their deeds in order for someone to justify their existence through praise.

———

So now let's take into account many of the opportunity costs of hiring one of these new six-figure administrators. For starters, how fast the board and superintendent are to allocate funds to pay for the new position is astonishing to say the least. Occasionally (depending on the state and school district) the base pay for the new admin position does not always crack the one hundred thousand dollar mark, but once you add in benefits that this person will be receiving along with that of their pay, then the six-figure cost barrier is not really all that difficult to break.

If you have children of your own, or even if you don't, you are probably very familiar with the fundraising aspect of public education. As you know, the majority of fundraising is done through selling something that is usually on the edible side consisting of a high sugar content which makes it very easy for the students to sell to other students, teachers, parents, or strangers while standing outside of a supermarket on a Sunday afternoon. And if seeing students of a public school system having to sell something to raise money upsets you, as it does many people, then look no further than the extra money spent on someone for that newly created administrative position. I'll get back to that topic in a little bit in the chapter *Selling Chocolate*.

The following are three examples where a fraction of the money put forth and approved by the local board of education to hire another six-figure administrative crony, or sending board members and administrators to multiple conferences throughout the year, or purchasing some educational program that was seen on some YouTube video, could be used to help those that it was originally intended to help.

Now before getting into the nuances of the activities that I'm about to mention, it is worth noting that coaches or teachers that offer to be at the helm of an after school activity are usually compensated in the form of a stipend at the end of the season or school year. These stipends vary quite a bit depending on the activity itself. Simply put—at least for the majority of the time—the more popular the activity or sport, the more money the coach or teacher (sometimes the coach is the teacher) will receive when they eventually get their check. The amount will also vary from one school to another so the numbers that I am using may not match those of a school in a different area, but that's beside the point.

Before getting into the money, it is important to note that not all coaches of a sport are a teacher at the school. Some coaches are not teachers at all and are hired by the school simply to coach. There are also others that coach at one school district and teach at another. I know—it's a mess.

Now let's take a look at some examples of people that do

put students first and, in many instances, end up paying out of pocket to do a job that many simply have no desire to undertake. Not only are they willing to put in the time and the effort, but when you do the math, the amount of money per hour is very low and wouldn't even compete with workers receiving minimum wage. It's actually, after all is said and done, less than that, and in some instances quite a bit less.

Let's use $2,500 as the average amount that the teacher or coach would receive after the activity is finished. I know of some instances where that number was much higher (varsity football coach for example was $4,000) than that and also some that were much lower. But on average, especially if you aren't one of the more popular sports or activities, this is about the amount those who I know that took on an extra assignment and work after school would receive before taxes. Now take off 25% of the $2500 for deductions—of which it will more than likely exceed 25%—and that leaves the coach or teacher with $1,875.

So now for a little arithmetic. Let's start with a three month long season (I am fully aware that this is short-changing them so feel free to adjust that number to match your given situation) and, erring on the conservative side, say that practice and games would only be a total of twenty hours per week. Once again, this is short-changing those of you who do this big time if you consider traveling, prep, and all of the other nuances of being a coach; but I'm just trying to keep the numbers simple so those not in education realize how much time and effort many put in for so little in return.

Finally, let's just use a four-week month time frame which would yield a total of eighty hours per month. Over a three month period, this would equate to a total of 240 hours invested into the players and the team. Let's add a couple of weeks in the summer for workouts or summer league or both, and go with only two hours a day for those practices or games. So two more weeks, not including weekends, at two hours a day for five days gives us twenty more hours for a total of 260 hours. Throw in two meetings with other coaches in the league (so add four more hours), a three hour CPR class, and this gives us a total of 267 hours; I'll go ahead and take that up to 270 hours (though I know for a fact from coaches who I know that 300 hours is pretty easy to do before breaking a sweat). Now take the $1,875 left over after taxes and divide that by 270 and you get... $6.94 per hour.

And this is just the break down per hour of time. Add in the gas money to run errands, the pizza parties for the players, and the helping out with a new pair of shoes because some of the players' families are financially strapped (many coaches are more than willing to help out a player in need), and you will find that many of these people end up in the red after all is said and done. All of this to coach for a school and administration that, unless they have a winning season, will not even know of the team's existence.

As promised, here are three example of people that really do put students first and also had a difficult time getting funding for things that are pretty much a necessity—such as soccer balls for a soccer team—for the activity to take place.

Example 1: A colleague coached the girls' varsity soccer team for a few years. He was easily exceeding the twenty hours per week as previously mentioned. Now you might think that a soccer coach would be supplied with an ample number of soccer balls for the team to utilize in practices and games, but you would be wrong. He had an extremely difficult time getting any funding for what was necessary for the team to practice and play. He actually had to go out and purchase a number of regulation balls (which weren't cheap) so that the team could practice and would also have the necessary balls to host their home games.

Yes, like so many sports and extracurricular activities, the team was selling boxes of chocolate, but it simply wasn't enough as there was literally no money in the budget for the team to get what was necessary to run the program.

This then led to the second problem that the coach faced: the uniforms. The uniforms that he inherited were extremely old and worn. So for the first few games, a number of players had to purchase t-shirts that had the colors of the school and used masking tape to put numbers on the shirts, seriously! And after weeks of trying to find funding and essentially begging for money for a soccer team that did not have soccer balls or uniforms, he [the coach] was finally able to get some money through one of the associations that wasn't directly related to school funding.

Example 2: Another colleague took the position of the junior varsity softball coach. And by the way, if you think getting money for a varsity sport was difficult, imagine the difficulty in obtaining the funds necessary for a junior varsity sport. Like so many in her shoes, she and her assistant would stay late to do their job and help out the players (many of which didn't even know what a cut-off person was).

One day she approached the principal about her assistant coach who was working for free and volunteering her time. She [the coach] inquired as to the possibility of a small stipend for the assistant coach. Understand that she did not need to do this (nor did the assistant coach expect this), but felt it would be a polite gesture to try and see if this was possible.

So to make a long story short, not only did the principal not even bother to try and find a means to help out the coach, she also told the coach that she [the coach] should take part of her own stipend and give it the assistant coach if she really felt that strongly about the assistant being compensated for her time. This suggestion came from a six-figure administrator that did not attend a single game for the entire season.

———

These were just two examples and both in the realm of athletics. Now imagine how tough it is to procure monies for some of the non-athletic (and usually less popular) after school programs. Whether it be the chess club, engineering and robotics club, or the Academic Decathlon team, many of these people do not receive a dime in the form of a compensation for what they do, and have a very difficult time just to find transportation to take the students to the competitions that go along with many of the clubs.

One thing to also understand is that both of these activities were coaching a specific sport which, as you know, only accounts for about a third of the school year in comparison to some activities which will run for the entire school year.

Example 3: This one is about a colleague who is in charge of the MESA (Math-Engineering-Science-Achievement) club for our school. This club takes many afterschool and weekend hours for building and planning. There are also a number of competitions throughout the year that are, in some cases, all day events. It is also a club that runs from the beginning of the school year until the end. Many of these MESA advisors also put hours in during the summer for fundraising and planning.

Now let's do a little math. The stipend for these positions (at least for the teachers I know of that are in charge of the program) is $2,000 for the year. Now subtract the 25% for deductions, and that leaves the advisor with $1,500. Since this is a year-round activity, let's use the standard 185 days in a school year, plus another ten for working in the summer. Now suppose that the people in charge work exactly one hour per day (I know for a fact that it's more but we'll just go with that) and you get 195 hours (I'll round that to 200 just because I know this is easily cheating them) for the year. After the division, we end up with $7.50 per hour. Now throw in a couple of pizza parties and those last second necessities for a competition that the advisor may or may not get reimbursed for, and you end up with a number that will be even lower.

Now some may argue that this is net pay and not gross pay and is a faulty argument. Okay fine, then just go with the gross pay instead which, for this person, would be $10 per hour. This number is less than minimum wage in the state of California, but also keep in mind that I erred on the side of caution when it comes to the number of hours that they put into the activity.

—

Gross or net pay isn't, however, the point. It is that these aforementioned people are really the ones who do put students first, and yet do not go around telling others in speeches how amazing they are at doing so. The majority of times the only people that go around talking about how they put students first are the ones that will put them first in order to receive praise about putting students first. These are usually the teachers or administrators that will send out an email (to all users, of course, including the superintendent) talking about how they partook in an activity such as going on a fieldtrip, and how this was somehow reflective of something that was talked about in the classroom.

Since we are on the subject, the people that send out the— *to all users*—emails are the same people in meetings that need to find a way to get others to focus their attention on them whenever the chance arises. In fact, they will do anything to get the attention away from the fact that very little learning, if any, goes on in the classroom. And just in case you didn't read my previous book, or even if you did, here is a reminder of that person.

Content Standard - Watch Roots Day 3
Language Standard - Write down 5 words from the movie

For another more detailed example of how the phrase *students first* is now all but meaningless, please read chapter 14: *Coach's Story*. This story demonstrates that regardless of the effectiveness of a teacher or coach (in this case both) with respect to the job that they are doing with the students, how easy it is to be removed from a coaching position if one of the cronies (who did his standard two years then left for a higher paying job) brought in by a sitting superintendent simply does not like you.

—

I have never once heard any teacher that puts the time and effort into their job, and really does put the students first, ever use the phrase that so many others have stated, but never really do, except for the purpose of recognition as well as to curry favor from peers and administration.

The three previous examples were of teachers that are in charge of a club or sport. There are lots more examples of these types of people in the education system, but let's not forget those who don't get paid at all for the extra hours that they put into their job. Those who show up well before contractual hours begin to meet with students—sometimes just a single student—who takes the bus to school, is dropped off early, and is in need of extra help. These teachers will not only arrive early to help out those who need it, but will also stay after school for an hour or two if the need arises. Whether that need is for help with that specific teacher's class, or the student just needs a place to hang out for a while because things aren't going so well with the home life.

We also need to include those who will go out of their way to buy a calculator, protractor, pencils, or even a laptop for certain students because some families simply cannot afford items that we take for granted. These are the teachers (more than you might think) whose actions go unnoticed that should be given the credit for putting students first and could easily be doing the touting, but don't.

So the next time you hear some administrator, or anyone for that matter, but especially administration, utter the words *students first* (regardless of whether you are in the field of education or just someone on the outside looking in) during some long-winded political speech, consider it to be no more than a *promesse da marinaio.*

- 3 -

The 21st Century Classroom

One of the biggest moves that many schools have made since the turn of the century is to try (and I say try, as many schools are still behind in technological advancements (not to mention the necessary infrastructure needed to support said advancements in the year 2018)) and purchase as much technology as financially possible in order to support the 21st century classroom.

The "quick and dirty" explanation of what this means: A 21st century classroom is essentially a classroom with all the necessary gadgets such as computers, Wi-Fi, and giant eighty-inch monitors (running the school about eight thousand dollars apiece) at the front of the class to enhance student learning. In other words, just another way for many lower performing schools to distract from the real issues that they face on a daily basis. As someone that works at one of these schools, I can honestly tell you that not only does all this technology not help or change the prevailing attitude of a typical student that attends the school, but in some respect, it has made teaching a more daunting task as teachers are expected to utilize and work miracles with it on a daily basis. After all, what good is it to spend hundreds of thousands (if not millions) of dollars on technology only to have it end up in a portable where it will collect dust; along with all of the other unused technology that the district paid for without first doing some due diligence to see if these purchases were even necessary.

The first problem of many is the pretense of a solution that Nouveau Administration puts on technology; as if it is the panacea that districts are looking for to solve the problems that have plagued them for decades now. And as obvious as it might be to some (mainly the people in the educational system who don't have the power to decide how funds are spent), putting monitors and access points in classrooms is not going to fix those generations of problems... although it will make for a good headline as well as photo op for administration. But in the mind of RAD, this time—under their leadership—is going to be different.

"It's not what is, it's what man thinks it is." – Larry Winzenread (High School History Teacher)

You have probably seen many articles for the last dozen or so years where multiple administrators, and maybe even some teachers, are interviewed about all of the technological changes (thanks to the passage of yet another thirty-year bond issuance) that are taking place at the schools within a district. And of course, all of these articles have pictures of students using some sort of new electronic device with a teacher standing next to said students all full of smiles as if everything is working out great. These articles will also include a picture of the *don't want to miss this photo op* superintendent who is simply padding his or her résumé for whatever school district they will end up working at once their current contract expires, and knows that a higher cell phone and car allowance awaits elsewhere.

The problem is that simply giving electronic devices to students is not going to fix the actual underlying problems that schools face on a day-to-day basis. All this act is doing is putting a band-aid on a broken leg, giving it a gentle kiss, and saying everything is now going to be fine; all the while hoping that no one on the outside looking in, or the reporter doing the article on the purchasing of the electronic devices, will come to the realization of this before those in charge of making the decisions to purchase the electronic devices have moved on to their next two-year stint.

The first thing to note is the rationale of pushing for all of this technology is done so for all the wrong reasons. Yes, we do live in the 21st century and most people walk around with a computer in their pocket with more capability than those we were using in the early 2000s. Laptops, tablets, smartphones, smart televisions, and voice recognition computers in our home that will order a pizza for us whenever we give the command are now the norm. But just because students have all of this technology and really don't know a life without it, doesn't necessarily mean that they are as technologically advanced as administration would like us to believe.

Doc Brown: *Great Scott! It's a tiny supercomputer. This must allow astrophysicists to triangulate complex equations in real time.*

Jimmy Kimmel: *Well, I guess it probably could do that, but mainly we use it to send little smiley faces to each other and to make plans; that sort of thing.*

(The Jimmy Kimmel Show, 2015)

The reality is that students and people in general just use their expensive phones as one would have used an agenda back in the '90s—with the exception that they can also take pictures and video and post it on social media for all to see within a few minutes. Let's not forget to mention that students today are also very good at using their electronic devices to cheat. They know how to find and download apps that allow them, for example, to take a picture of a linear equation which will give them the steps and the answer almost immediately.

On that note, if you are a teacher, isn't it amazing how some students will have the latest $700 smartphone or a $150 pair of shoes, but never show up to class with a backpack, some sort of writing utensil, or just paper to write on. And when you ask them why they don't have any of the basics, their excuse is usually along the lines of: *because those things are too expensive.*

The logic that students today are more advanced when it comes to technology because they know how to use the most current and available technology is, as usual when it comes to most administrative logic, faulty at best. A person is not advanced at something because they know how to use whatever that something is just like everyone else does; that is usually what is referred to as being average. But then again, in this *everyone gets a trophy for doing anything era*, then calling someone advanced for just knowing the basics seems apt.

"Trophies, so that's the easy answer!" – Luann Van Houten (The Simpsons)

Another issue (probably the biggest when it comes to utilizing these electronic devices) with giving out electronic devices and putting in new computer labs, is that the infrastructure of many of these schools is so old that they cannot support the devices that are being handed out. Many of the schools will find quick and cheap workarounds that somewhat patch up the problems. These patches, however, are merely a temporary fix as the issues with students and staff using the technology will only become more problematic as the demands of the district grid continue to increase.

Here is but one example as to how RAD simply does not understand how to bring technology into a district that neither has the infrastructural support, or the manpower, to build and sustain that which is necessary for all of the technology that the district wants to incorporate. As usual, they are only concerned with the attention that it will bring once the local newspaper catches wind of what the district is going to purchase for the students.

Circa 2010, the superintendent of the school district that I work for was adamant about bringing iPads and Surface Pros to the school. Keep in mind that the school had very little wireless capability at that moment—definitely not enough to support the thousands of devices that the district envisioned—and this was only talk about getting the process started. There were many meetings with teachers and tech support as to what steps should be taken in order to build up the technological infrastructure; the logical first step to support the purchasing of a number of tablets for students to use, and to also handle more technology in the future. Many ideas were thrown around and everyone at the meetings agreed that it was important that every school in the district first be upgraded in order to support a 21st century classroom before making any hardware and software purchases. This of course, would be accomplished financially through yet another bond issuance that was recently passed (as is with every new superintendent, by the way).

During one of the meetings, it was explained to the superintendent that it might be a better idea for the district to create a cloud so that they would not have to spend more money purchasing individual towers; which were still being used in any classroom that was lucky enough to have computers and in each of the computer labs. It was also stressed how much time and money could be saved if the district went to the cloud so the one part-time site tech would not have to spend the majority of his time on the campus fixing the problems of each individual computer tower; which was essentially how he spent his four hours a day on campus. We also explained to the superintendent that if the district just went out and purchased tablets, the issues would be the same and the already busy part-time tech person would also have to fix the daily problems with the proposed purchase of forty iPads and forty Surface Pros.

But even though the superintendent and everyone agreed that purchasing the tablets should not be the first thing on the list, they were the first things that were purchased by the district superintendent. So why do the thing first that everyone agreed should have been the last thing done? As I've mentioned, admin simply can't pass up a photo op. The two carts of tablets were put together just in time for a visit from the superintendent of California public schools (Torlakson). When he arrived for his visit, there would be two classrooms of students with a cart of tablets for them to use. And just like every other time a school purchases and begins to use these devices, there just happens to be a reporter from the local newspaper on site to take pictures of the students using them for whatever the assignment was for that day.

In other words, we had multiple meetings to discuss what the best course of action was for the school, and all agreed that purchasing the tablets would not have been the wisest investment for the district to make, but in the end, that did not seem to matter. The superintendent, as always, has the final say in the decision making process. The iPads and Surface Pros were then purchased for yet another shameless act of improving the district image.

And as you probably already guessed, it took the students less than a day to figure out a way to get around the firewall and access pornography on the devices. It was also less than a week before the students realized that the devices were not assigned to any individual student and that they could just walk out of the classroom with a tablet and no one would be the wiser. So where are these two carts of tablets today? They are still around, but rarely used. And although both carts are almost full when it comes to the number of devices, they are not all the original devices that were there from the first day. Many have had to be replaced simply because no one has really been keeping track of the location of devices that were there on the first day of use.

The reason that they are not used as often is that no one really understood how to use them as a teaching apparatus. The teachers were simply given the tablets just in time for the visit from the California Superintendent of Public Instruction. Some apps were thrown on them to make it look as if this is finally the miracle that this one particular school has been waiting for. Alas, for anyone with a little common sense—which is not so common—would know, throwing technology at a school and expecting it to fix generations of problems is wishful thinking to say the least.

"I'd sooner trust in great teachers with mediocre tools, than mediocre teachers with great tools." – J. Eichinger

There was never any discussion about how the tablets would be kept up-to -date with all the newest software and how just standard maintenance of the devices would take up the majority of each day for the one part-time tech person on campus. All that mattered was that the district superintendent at the time was able to get a picture of himself in the local newspaper along with the California Superintendent of Public Instructions for yet another star to add to his résumé. And the school itself still did not have the infrastructure necessary to support more devices and computer labs. In fact, the tablets themselves were not running off of the district internet. Each cart had its own access point that could only support the tablets that were in the cart. In other words, get the devices and manufacture some sort of means for them to access the internet just in time for Torlakson's visit.

What really made maintenance difficult on these gadgets, being that the district cloud was still at least five years away, was that when a problem did occur (which was almost immediately and daily), the one part-time person in charge of technology for the school site would have to take the physical gadget out of the cart in which it was stored, figure out what the exact problem was, and possibly do an entire factory restore of the item which, if you are familiar with computer maintenance, is not exactly an instantaneous process.

Now for those of you thinking ah... this must be the Los Angeles Unified School District and their iPad fiasco going back to 2013. Alas, it is not. I can assure you that Los Angeles Unified is just one of many school districts that jumped on the tablet bandwagon. The reason that other school districts with similar iPad issues don't show up in the news in the same manner as LA Unified, is simply that the majority of school districts across the country are much smaller in size and do not deal in the magnitude of dollars as that of LA Unified. This keeps smaller school districts under the media radar when it comes to the ineffectiveness of the purchased technology and how the money spent did not yield the ROI (Return on Investment) as those making and approving the decision to purchase the devices had envisioned.

Now that I think about, it would be quite nice for the local newspaper that writes these articles to begin with to do a follow-up after a couple of years to see how cost effective these purchases were, and how they have assisted in student learning. Then again, there really would not be much of a follow-up story as the people who originally put this plan into action would be long gone.

And yes, he was gone, but actually a little less than two years later.

The following superintendent—who had the position for about a year as a puppet for the board majority (and I cannot stress enough how clueless this person was when it came to technology)—also did not do what was necessary to get the schools updated to where they should be electronically. It wasn't until the more recent superintendent who started in 2013 that the district began to update what was necessary to get the schools in the district into the 21st century. And this was only because of the Common Core exams (which are all done online) were starting to take place. If it wasn't for the adoption of these exams by the state, then more than likely the schools in this district would still be where they were in the late '90s and early '00s.

So before you go thinking *ah, so there is a superintendent that did help improve and have a positive impact on the district,* this was also the same superintendent that brought in all of his cronies and gave them all either an assistant superintendent, principal, or vice principal job regardless of whether or not they were qualified. The principal of the middle school that was hired was the same one that had to be transferred half way through his second year after losing control of every aspect of the school which, by the way, isn't usually enough to be removed as an administrator (unless there is an act that merits an investigation such as locking a student in a closet (just search: "principal (or teacher) locks student in closet," and you might be surprised at how many hits you get... then again maybe not)). If it wasn't for the complaining parents at the board meetings (yes, there were teachers also complaining, but that never means anything in the eyes of the board or superintendent), this principal would never have been removed and more than likely would still be in charge of the school.

This is the same person that was mentioned in *The Need For Common Core* who told students during the first assembly that their job as students is to "[H]ave fun", and that "[G]rades don't matter until the fourth quarter", which goes to show how little he knew about the site of which he was in charge; as this particular middle school is on the trimester system and not the quarter system. He was also (according to everyone on the interview panel with the exception of his friend, the superintendent) the worst candidate for the job and finished in last place when it came to ranking the interviewees.

—

The problem with creating and putting so much emphasis

on a 21st century classroom is that many administrators are absolutely clueless about what is really necessary for students' success. The assumption has always been that somehow all of this expensive equipment and software are paradigm shifting and will somehow fix everything even though many of them simply do not understand the how it all works.

Peggy: *Now this machine is going to wind up saving us money in the long run.*

Al: *How? Does it emit powerful life-draining radiation?*

Peggy: *Well I don't know. I don't even know how to use it. I don't even know why we need it. I just know I want it.*

(Married with Children)

Here is an email I received from the principal asking—or maybe telling me as I'm not really sure how to interpret what was written with the question mark at the end—why I wasn't using [*software name*] (omitted because it could be any piece of paid-for software) with my AP class because the district had purchased a multi-year subscription which was apparently expensive:

"*We are getting critique by the DO with [insert software name here]. They know who is using and who does not. Please support this expensive tool for our students that the district is sponsoring?*" – RAD

For starters (setting aside the fact that there are clearly syntactical problems with the email), no one really asked any of the teachers if this software would work for their classes. They [being the person or persons at the district office in charge of making these decisions without teacher input] decided that this would be good for the Advanced Placement classes as a teaching and review tool. And although some teachers did use it occasionally for review purposes, just about every AP teacher—

with the exception of the standard sycophant—agreed that it was not as good as the district was making it out to be and used it only occasionally.

Many teachers, especially the ones doing this type of class long enough, already have more than enough materials to assist with teaching the class. The teachers that did use it agreed that it was nice, but that many students would just copy each other when doing the assignments; but the district and the principal simply did not care. They made this purchase without any input from the AP teachers and just assumed that everything the teachers were already using was just going to be pushed aside to use this "expensive tool".

It's fairly common practice for this to happen. The main reason (although this will never be admitted) is that both district and site administration need to show that they are being "progressive" (*progressive* being the new hyped and overused word that seems to be taking the place of the phrase *paradigm shift*) in their thinking, and that student learning will grow exponentially because of the money that is being ~~wisely spent~~ wasted on some new technology that is currently all the rave.

"Why would they put all that money into a thing with red lights the keep going back and forth? Doesn't make any sense." – Commander Buck Murdock (Airplane 2: The Sequel, 1982)

And despite all of these "expensive tools" the school district has paid for along with that of new computer labs, laptop carts, eighty-inch touch-screen monitors up in front of the classrooms (and an accompanying forty-inch monitor in the back of a few selected classrooms), the standardized test results of this school, and similar schools in the area taking the same approach to improving student learning, have not changed.

The school does brag about its twenty to thirty percent

passing rate when it comes to AP test results, though. Now you might be thinking: *that's actually pretty good for an inner-city high school;* and if you only went by the overall percentage then you might be right. But anyone with a basic understanding of statistics knows full well that an overall percentage, although may look good on paper, does not really tell much of a story. If you were to break the percentage down to individual classes, you would find that the only reason the overall percentage of passing is so high is because of the AP Spanish Language exam.

Almost every student that takes AP Spanish Language class passes the corresponding exam. But when you look at the demographics of the area and realize that about ninety-five percent of the student population has Spanish as the main language spoken in the home, then this result is not very surprising. But if you were to remove this result from the total, you would find that percent passing is much, much lower. I'll get back to this discussion a little later in the chapter *Public Perception.*

The point is that all of this technology and the "expensive tools" that the district is purchasing with bond money are simply not helping. All it is doing is creating a slight-of-hand act to get people to look somewhere else while the underlying problems of the school not only remain, but in many instances are getting worse.

As a side note, I want to plug phet.colorado.edu (no, I am not tied to them in any way and they are not paying me to do this). If you teach a science class then you are more than likely familiar with not only the interactive tutorials, but the open source assignments that many teachers using Phet upload and add to the teaching resources library. And—wait for it—it's 100% free. In fact, there are a number of free sites out there to cover almost all bases of education. Most people don't consider, for example, YouTube as a good educational resource, but it really is. Kaotix.com and desmos.com are free math websites that I have used many times with my algebra students. But do administrators ever ask the teachers what resources we are using before making these "expensive tool" purchases? Rarely, and even when they do ask, it is usually some teacher from their sycophantic inner circle who will always agree with whatever administration decides.

Colleagues and I have used these sites many times and it is a great example of how little administration knows about what's out there that doesn't cost the district a dime. Then again, this would require district administration to admit that they don't know something; and when it comes to RAD, admitting that there is something that they do not know is simply out of the question.

Now imagine how much money the district would save if they cut back on just a few of these purchases and put the money towards new instruments for the band, or soccer uniforms so the players don't have to tape their number onto the back of a t-shirt to make it look like an official school uniform. But even if that did happen, the probability of these monies making it to where it is needed the most if districts did cut spending on some of these products is almost zero. I would go so far as to say there is a much greater probability of proving that either P equals NP, or P does not equal NP, long before the money that administrators get their hands on first ever makes it to where it is supposed to go.

———

The fantasy of technology fixing generations of problems at schools, in districts, and within a community is the current approach that the school boards which represent said districts—especially lower performing ones—are constantly taking to try and fix a cultural mentality in a standard two-year time frame. Yes, it does provide (as I have said many times) for a nice photo op as well as a distraction from what is really going on, or not, within the walls of the school. But as long as these decisions are left in the hands of administrators—many of which do not reside in the district or, in many cases, were even aware of the district's existence until they were interviewed for the job—then these are the types of decisions that we can expect until real change comes about. These are the people who work in an office that never has an issue with temperature control; where it is warm in the winter and cool in the summer.

"Don't be too proud of this technological terror you've constructed." - Darth Vader (Star Wars Episode IV—A New Hope, 1977)

Now before thinking that I am somehow anti-technology in the classroom I can assure you I am not. I am, however, not a fan of the amount of money that is wasted on purchasing things (be they electronic devices, or anything that administration thinks that the school sites in the district need, before consulting those people that could tell them more definitively) that are simply not necessary as well as the dependence on technology to fix problems overnight.

—

During an in-service day at the beginning of this school year, the math teachers in the department had to attend a technology training—from the company whose books we just spent tens of thousands of dollars to purchase—on how to use their software as well as other websites that may complement their books. Each teacher in that room has at least fifteen years of teaching under their belt. Of course, that does not imply that each of the teachers is technologically savvy and knows how to use certain websites or apps in order to assist in student learning. But at least for this instance, that was not the case. All of us have been using certain sites and technology (the most popular ones we use the most are, coincidently, free) for a number of years. If you have been using the internet in your classroom for a few years, then you also know which sites are good, which ones are mediocre, and those that are just awful. Long story short (as I won't bore you with the torturous details of sitting through a training where the presenter is only showing you things that you are already familiar with), and there is probably a chance that this has happened to you, we ended up helping the presenter understand not only certain aspects of the websites and apps that he was there to demonstrate to us, but we also showed him a number of free sites that we have been using for years (he had no idea about www.wolframalpha.com).

After the morning session finally came to an end, we all broke for lunch. I was the first person to return to the room after lunch and the presenter was already there. We started to discuss the dependency that a growing number of school districts have when it comes to technology being the panacea for that which ails. He was very candid (I don't think he would have been had the rest of the group been there) about how schools like ours spend hundreds of thousands of dollars to buy technology in the hopes that it will fix all of the problems that the district is having. He also mentioned how he had done similar training for schools that aren't obsessed with going one-to-one (one laptop or tablet for each student) and only have computer labs for their students.

The one item that the presenter shared with me (which would be surprising to all RADs) is that schools that do not have a dependence on technology are the ones whose students are outperforming when it comes to whatever is currently in vogue to help students with standardized testing. Needless to say that I was somewhat perplexed, but also very happy that he was so forthcoming when it came to how much money school districts throw at technology in the hopes that somehow these purchases are going to cure everything.

Secretary: *Mr. Escalante, Mr. Escalante, did you hear the news? We got the computers!*

Jaime Escalante: *Yep, that'll do it.*

(Stand and Deliver, 1988)

The presenter was also very forthright when it came to the cost of the training that we had to sit through for that day. Although I was not able to get a number as to the cost, you have to figure that he had to fly in from another state to do a full day training, and that there was to be a follow-up a few months later—of which I just happened to be sick that day, so I sadly had to miss that session. I would estimate that the two days of training would easily have cost the district at least three thousand dollars (I would in no way be surprised if it was double that amount) for something that we already knew. Maybe if the those planning these in-service days would have simply taken the time to ask us whether or not we needed this particular "training", we could have saved some money and worked on something useful such as articulating with the middle school teachers on what we could do to help prepare students for both high school and, if it's in their future, some sort of post-secondary education. Then again, that would have made sense.

This addiction to technology really just needs to stop. So much money is being thrown at this device or that piece of software with very little understanding when it comes to the efficacy of what it is that the money is being used to purchase.

And as long as the administrators in charge keep making decisions to buy whatever piece of technology or software is the most fashionable at some given time—not to mention bringing in the most favorable of headlines when it comes to the local newspaper or some other means of public relations—then this wasting of taxpayer dollars will only continue.

As I mentioned earlier, I am not anti-technology as it does have its place in the classroom as well as in our lives on a daily basis. But school districts really need to take a step back in thinking when it comes to passing bonds off on the local homeowners or renters (as the owners will more than likely pass any increase in their mortgage payment onto those renting their home) in order to purchase more tablets, laptops, or the all-in-one computers. Let's also not forget about all the other accessories needed to work with these items such as routers, printers, and of course, the underpaid and undervalued tech people (I mean that in the sincerest way as no school would be able to function without them) that go from class to class in order to help us when a piece of our tech is not working properly.

So the next time you read an article from a school district that boasts about all of the new and amazing technology being bought and placed into the classroom to improve student learning, or you are invited to a showing of all of this new technology by the superintendent, just remember that many (if not all) of these decisions to use taxpayer money to purchase hundreds of thousands of dollars of equipment were made by a small handful of people on a committee that have no idea how any of it is going to be used, and are absolutely clueless as to whether or not it will shift the paradigm when it comes to student learning.

- 4 -

Exploiting the Glitches

It's no secret that people in general prefer to try and find a fast and simple solution to a problem that they might be up against. Everyone, including me, is guilty of doing this at one time or another. This is becoming even more prevalent (especially in the field of education) with immediate access to information the likes of which mankind has only been privy to for the last twenty-five years—give or take a few.

Marge: *Homer, what are you doing?*

Homer: *Listen, do you want the job done right, or do you want it done fast?*

Marge: *Well like all Americans, fast!*

(The Simpsons)

But the path through the K–12 system is getting to the point where it is just too easy to make it through and get that high school diploma. After four years of high school, when all is said and done, receiving the diploma is pretty much a given. When schools get to that stage where the graduation rates are increasing every year and nearly everyone is graduating, then what is the intrinsic value of that diploma? More importantly, what does it mean now that there are vast numbers of graduates who are reading and writing at what is measured as a sixth-grade level? Perhaps you might be thinking that recent upward trends in graduation rates across the country are due to academic rigor and students being at, or even above grade level, and that somehow their critical thinking and problem solving skills are a reflection of that increase. Then again, if you did believe that, then you probably wouldn't be this far into the book to begin with.

Students realize at a very young age how simple it is to get from one grade to the next as long as they show up every now and again as well as occasionally turn in some work. The students know that they will be promoted to the next level regardless of how much, or little, they actually learned. It doesn't take too long for them to realize that being held back is something that they never have to worry about; thanks to the egregious amount of paperwork to do so, the act of being held back—at least more than once—is all but obsolete.

Here is actual language from California Education Code when it comes to PPR (Pupil Promotion and Retention):
Existing law requires the governing board of each school district and each county superintendent of schools to adopt policies regarding pupil promotion and retention, and requires a pupil to be promoted or retained only as provided according to those policies.

So if you were ever wondering why some schools seem to have a nearly one-hundred percent pupil promotion rate despite these "advancing" students being below grade level (in some instances by several, up to and including complete illiteracy) when it comes to whatever metrics the school district uses to measure student learning, there you have it. The board of education simply does not want to look bad in the eyes of the people that they are counting on to re-elect them to the position that they currently hold. And with no form of accountability when it comes to graduating (California tried it for about seven years before deciding that it wasn't producing the desired results), all a student needs to do to ~~earn~~ get a diploma is complete a watered-down version of a class in order to walk down the aisle with their peers in June to the tune of "Pomp and Circumstance" by Edward Elgar, regardless of the questionable value or specifics of either, respectively.

Let me stop here and once again emphasize that not every school is guilty of committing this type of manipulation. But more schools are jumping on the bandwagon of making it easier to compete for more students to attend their school in order to keep, and hopefully increase, the amount of funding that is received each year. Meanwhile, the charter-school competition that forces parents to try and "select" the best educational option for their greatest hopes instead of relying on the increasingly questionable public education system (see how this is a self-feeding system?) only incentivizes the promise of guaranteeing a child's graduation, much like for-profit universities who, it might be added, have been increasingly shut down as diploma-mills.

At what point do schools simply have students check-in at the beginning of their ninth-grade year, then just show up four years later to pick up their diploma? The question is obviously jocular, but are we really that far off from this happening? And if that be the case, then why wait four years? Since many schools are constantly lowering the bar a little more every year, why not just have the new freshmen students sign up on the first day of school, then walk down the aisle and pick-up their diploma the same day as enrolling? I know that sounds a little far-fetched, but as you'll read about in a moment (or you have been doing this long enough), it really isn't.

A friend of mine works at a school that is similar to that of my own when it comes to the demographics and revolving door administration. During a three-week summer school session a couple of years ago, a student made up one hundred and eighty-five credits in just three weeks through online credit-recovery classes. After doing a little bit of arithmetic, that came to about seventy percent of the number of units required to graduate.

For emphasis, this student barely showed up at all during their first three years of high school. On top of that, when the student did show up to class, they made very little, if any, attempt to participate in any of the classes (although the student rarely attended classes when on campus). And after three years of doing this, they were able to catch-up to the rest of the class in just three weeks of summer school. This student, by the way, is the only one that I know of who made up that many credits in such a short amount of time. And even though this is an extreme case, I can assure you that making up a high percentage of missing credits in a short amount of time is not an isolated incident.

If you aren't in education then it's important to note that it is not atypical for a senior that is missing (in some instances at least an entire year's worth) credits needed to graduate to make them up in a short amount of time. Though this process varies as to when it starts, from my own experience it is usually around the end of April or the first week of May with about a month left in the school year. This is usually the time of year when panic mode kicks in for both the students in danger of not graduating, as well the administrators who are worried about those students in danger of not graduating, but for different reasons. Though they might pretend it's about the students, they do not care about a student graduating so much as the data-point that the student represents on the graph of the school's graduation rate. This is also the time when these last-minute, credit-recovery shenanigans start to take place.

With online credit recovery classes rapidly becoming the means for students to make up any missing credits, many are realizing that simply attending classes isn't necessary as they will be given many opportunities to ~~earn~~ get any missing credits through one of these online programs. As more students complete their schooling in this manner, the more other students will likely take the same path as they find yet another crack in the system.

However, online recovery classes are simply the current method of making up a slew of credits in a short amount of time. This idea of making up units necessary in an abbreviated timeframe has been going on for as long as I have been in education, both as a teacher and a student. Without getting into the minutia, before all of the online credit-recovery programs, students who were very much behind the rest of their class and in danger of not graduating would have attended adult school, or be enrolled into an independent study program in order to make up the number of units necessary for graduation. Granted, it was a little slower, but this act of miraculously completing the necessary classes with just a few weeks left in the school year isn't exactly anything new to the educational system.

If a student has a special education designation with accompanying IEP (or 504, if no diagnosable disorder is determined but the parents just really insists on their child being given" modifications"), there are a number of packets that can be completed which will stand as equivalent to having completed a semester of study in any given course. This is certainly true in California, though I can't claim to know how it translates to other states (though it seems that given the demand for adaptation to all students' needs, it would likely be nationwide). Therein lies the question: If we can reduce the curriculum to a number of short-response and multiple-choice tests, then why not offer that option to every student who wishes to ~~earn~~ get their diploma through this method?

You think there is an administrative answer to this, don't you? There isn't. Because no matter how decisively a school takes efforts to prevent such reduction of a diploma to a giant multiple-choice test, it's a question of how determined the student, their parent(s), counselors, and vice principals want this student to ~~earn~~ get a diploma, and their teachers have very little to do with the overall equation unless they happen to teach seniors. In most cases, this means that those who are unforgiving will not receive senior classes. That's something that cannot be avoided, because the master schedule at any site is purely at the discretion of the principal regardless of education, training, or even credentials, although in extreme cases it might be investigated. That's the reality of the situation at most schools, and it's something that enables the manipulation to the means by which students complete the necessary credits to continue the increase of the graduation rates as much as anything else. Within any system, the most common path to the endpoint is the one of least resistance.

—

Before continuing, we all know that there are plenty of students that do not take the path of least resistance. The problem is that these types of students are more and more becoming the exception rather than the rule. I want to give an example of one such student that not only took the path of most resistance, but also forced herself to take more challenging classes even though her interest in some of those classes was, well... there really wasn't any. She took them solely to challenge herself and also understood that she might need what she learned from them later on in life.

I once had a student who wanted to be a lawyer and had no interest in pursuing a career in the math or science fields. But even though her heart was in the field of Political Science, she still took AP Chemistry and AP Calculus even though, at the time, she had absolutely no interest in going into areas to which taking these classes and tests would eventually lead. But she took them anyway, and even though she struggled, she also knew that taking challenging classes would only benefit her in the long run.

She was definitely an extremely tough student. During her four years in high school, she challenged an administration that was trying to eliminate certain AP classes from the schedule for the usual reason; the classes were too small and it's more cost effective to have a teacher with thirty-six students in a general class than fifteen in an AP class. The results of her actions saved these classes and also got her story and her picture on the front page of the local newspaper, which I still have today.

Fast forward about seven years (the situation I just mentioned took place during the start of her junior year in high school) and she ended up with a degree from Berkeley. I honestly don't know what field of study her degree is in, but what I do know is that she has been working for Google ever since.

"It is our failure to become our perceived ideal that ultimately defines us and makes us unique." – Conan O'Brien (Dartmouth College Commencement Address, 2011)

As many of you know, it is very rare that the future we had planned in our youth turns out to be our reality. This young lady is an example of someone who took classes in order to be challenged even though she originally had no intentions of doing anything in the field of technology. And yet, here she is many years later working for one of the largest tech companies in the world.

And just to emphasize how resilient this young lady is, if you thought taking on RAD while being a high school student was tough (and if you have dealt with RAD, you know exactly how difficult that can be), she was also diagnosed with cervical cancer in her late teens or early twenties. I honestly don't know the exact time when this did happen, as she did not exactly convey her condition aside from immediate family and those closest to her. When I did find out about her condition, I sent her an email telling her that if cancer knew who they were going up against, that it wouldn't have bothered. Needless to say she won, and recently gave birth to her first child—a girl.

By the way, for those of you wondering how and why teachers put up with RAD's nonsense, and all of the other things that I have written about, it's because of the few and far between stories like hers that help to make this job a little more tolerable.

———

If you are part of Gen X or earlier, you probably remember the days of the super-senior. These were students who didn't have all of their credits upon graduation and would attend classes on campus (at least at the school that I attended) until they fulfilled the minimum requirements to get their diploma. These students would attend class with the rest of the student population until they earned the credits that were needed. Once they did earn their credits, they received their diploma and moved on.

With social media being as it is, students are fully aware (through word-of-messaging on social media) that they are going to be promoted to the next level regardless of how much effort, or lack thereof, they put into a class. Of course, there are students who understand that taking the easy path to graduation is not always beneficial to their future, but even those that try to challenge themselves are more often than not equaled and rivaled by those who show up, sit in a seat, get their credits, and eventually ~~earn~~ stumble upon their diploma.

The origins of this trend are almost Shakespearean in their levels of dramatic irony, too. Let us take a trip in the way-back machine to "No Child Left Behind," c. 2000. (George W. Bush's administration) which, to carry us into the new millennium, would seek to censure the "social promotion" that had become endemic to the public education system, and which would establish clear and demonstrable "Standards" for educators to assess and implement in terms of measurable outcomes toward "mastery".

Meanwhile, this established a system of "API" (Academic Performance Index) that was relied upon as a literal point of objective evaluation in terms of whether or not any student would receive a "good education", regardless of that student's individual interest in general education in the first place, and which meant that, because part of API was the graduation rate of an institution (measured along an index of standardized test scores, of course), there became a literal incentive to socially promote students (as is done literally without question until high school in the first place, at least in California—I defy you to find someone who has been held back in middle school in California, and if so, it's a story that has to be worth telling).

Since colleges begin to look at student performance at the 9th/10th grade (depending on whether you want to focus on the "overall" or "academic" GPA, which admissions officers have the discretion of doing at their seemingly sovereign levels of judgment, which are so far beyond transparency that we have stopped questioning them) in terms of what "counts" insofar as academic performance is concerned, middle school seems to be nothing more than a test of emotional fortitude, and if you have ever had the experience of teaching it... you probably know it might be not the most inaccurate way to deal with it.

That's neither here nor there, though—the reality is that a butt load (this is actually a vintner's unit of measurement equal to 48 bushels of wine, so don't get all haughty) of seniors have the opportunity to enroll in a number of courses that require them to merely click buttons and eventually receive the same lambskin as the Valedictorian, in terms of actual face-value. Can anyone really blame any of them for taking that option if it is presented to them? Of course, it never is... explicitly. It's always a matter of rumor and whisper about how easy so-and-so is and how you can just this-and-that. But it's the same at every school, and as long as graduation rates are on the rise, everyone just smiles and carries on. Teachers' grades are nullified at the last minute, and there's nothing they can really do about it if enough counselors and VPs are ready to declare that alternate methods of assessment were taken to determine sufficient mastery of the objective curriculum. That's what an objectively measurable curriculum means, after all, as RAD will remind you with every request for a pivot-chart that demonstrates student growth, or a "data wall" that displays the performance on district or state benchmarks your students have demonstrated, regardless of what it looks like. The numbers don't lie—and the less you know about their actually meaning, the better.

This is essentially the same means by which education deals with teachers. All teachers know that once they are high enough on the seniority list once their tenure is achieved, that there really is no way for the district to let them go; this barring some sort of egregious act with a student which then allows the district to release a teacher (and even then it can be a difficult process). Teachers know that the system does not care how about what they or their students accomplish in the classroom, but if you are the last one in, you're also the first one out regardless of how effective you might be with your students. Though the majority of teachers will work hard until that last day when they turn in their keys for one last time, there are those who will take advantage of the tenure and seniority glitch in the system that allows them to cruise into retirement (see page 292).

Nathan Drake: *It's not going to be easy, you know.*

Elena Drake: *Nothing worthwhile is.*

(Uncharted 4: A Thief's End, 2016)

Back in the early 2000s, our school had an exchange student from Egypt. When he arrived, he had a pretty reserved personality and also had very good work habits (many of you already know not only where this is going, but also how it ends). He was enrolled in my Honors Pre-Calculus class (which the school no longer offers) which wasn't exactly a walk in the park. From the beginning of the class, he had exhibited a very good understanding of mathematics and had a strong foundation, which lead to an A for the first quarter—not exactly an easy feat.

But as the school year progressed, his grade in the class began to falter. His personality also began to change, as his initial reserved persona started to morph into that of an outgoing one. This type of metamorphosis isn't necessarily a bad thing, per se, but usually a change in personality and a drop in grades go hand-in-hand. This is when he started to struggle in my class; and by the end of the semester, the A that he had earned for the first quarter had turned into a C.

When second semester began, he made no effort to try and revert back to his initial personality when it came to his work habits. As a matter of fact, those work habits continued to go in the wrong direction. He started to do less when it came to homework which lead to a drop in both quiz and test scores. By the time the second semester was about half way over, that C had turned into a D and was deteriorating very rapidly. He was completing very little homework at this junction, and he also began to have attendance problems.

When I asked him about his missing homework and the issue with attendance, he was very honest and said that he had been [*insert school name here*]-ized. He added that he was getting A's and B's in almost all of his other classes for doing very little or any work at all. The student was very candid and admitted that he simply did not want to do any work with only one quarter left in the school year. His only real concern was the reaction from his parents (both of whom are doctors back in Egypt) when they found out about his F in the class. But there didn't exactly appear to be any sense urgency or anxiety when he brought that up. At least the school didn't take away his sense of honesty; although I do believe it would have had he stayed around for another year.

Let's review: An exchange student whose parents are both doctors is transformed from a hard-working reserved student, to one that has the typical attitude of many of the students on campus in less than a one semester time frame. The one difference between his personality and the majority of students on campus is that he accepted full responsibility for his final grade being what it was. He had no desire to try and blame anyone else which, if you're a teacher, is somewhat confusing as the majority of students will usually try to blame anyone else for their failure—especially the teacher.

———

A student taking the easiest route to graduation is something that shouldn't shock anyone. Many students would rather sit in a class that takes very little effort, if any at all, to receive a high mark than take a challenging class that they might get something out of.

One instance I will briefly mention again from my previous book is the AP science class that fills up every year and then some. So let's do a brief examination as to why that happens. Before doing so, it is important to understand that the required reading for this course is extremely difficult and really is a reflection of a college level textbook. And yet, the majority of students in the class are English Language Learners (ELLs). For the up-and-coming school year, the number of requests for this AP class was over one hundred students. Although that might not sound like a lot, that number represents about ten percent of the students enrolled at the school.

One more point to add (pun intended) is that because the class mentioned is an AP class, then each grade counts as one point higher for a student's grade point average. So a C in that class would be equivalent to a B from a general class. This is one more reason students like to take classes like these. Not only does it require very little work to pass, but it also boosts their GPA because of that one extra point—which makes the transcripts for the students that take the class look that much nicer.

But not all the students would get an A on the unit exams, which is why some students didn't get an A at the end of the semester. So how is it possible that a student can get an exam ahead of time and not get an A on it? Well, the answer choices were shuffled. I mean it wouldn't be an AP class if there wasn't some sort of challenge to it, right?

The eye-opening part of this to a new and inexperienced teacher, or someone that is not part of the everyday educational experience, is that this teacher will be praised as a "good" teacher by both students and administration alike because of the grades that the students are given at the end of the semester.

"My old math teacher was really good because he would do the homework problems on the board for us." – Transfer Student explaining to me why her previous teacher did a better job at teaching math than I was doing.

You might, or maybe not, be surprised at what traits that students, and some people in general, use to pass judgment as to what characteristics make a "good" teacher. Because the previously mentioned AP teacher (as well as others) only gave the students A's, B's, and the occasional C, they were celebrated as a "good" teacher because no student received anything below a C for the class.

Now you might be thinking that only passing grades for an AP class, but no passing grades for the actual AP exam, might raise some red flags to administration about the students in the class learning the content as stipulated by the College Board. Alas, that would not be the case. As long as the students pass the class, then the disconnect between the AP scores and the grades will be completely overlooked.

See, RAD doesn't really care about what teacher is best suited for any specific job. They care about which teacher will pass the most students, thereby keeping the graduation rate up near that horizontal asymptote of one hundred percent. You might think that learning should take precedence over grades, but you would be wrong for the majority of schools and districts across the country.

—

A friend (different from the friend and district mentioned a few pages back) works at a neighboring district that is pretty much identical to mine when it comes to the demographics. The student body of the school is about ninety-five percent Hispanic where the primary language spoken in the home is Spanish. He also has students in his class that speak very little English—if any at all.

One day, the superintendent and a couple of cronies from the district office—along with the school's principal—decided to grace a few classrooms with their presence. They walked through my friend's classroom and the very first question the top RAD asked of a student was, "*What is your grade?*"

The one detail that really made the visit and the question a classic work of comedy—which goes along with something we say almost every day at lunch with respect to making up this kind of stuff—was that the student didn't speak any English, and didn't understand the question that was being asked. And since RAD didn't speak any Spanish, the student just kind of sat there and stared. So instead of trying to bridge the gap as it was very evident that this had made the RAD a little uncomfortable, they decided to just pretend it didn't happen and walked over to the next table to ask a different student the exact same question. Looks like all that knowledge attained by that administrative credential and master's degree in education is not exactly paying off for this person (well it is, but only in the sense of how much this person is paid as opposed to how much they know about what goes on in the classroom).

You might think that RAD would have something more imaginative to ask, or maybe speak even just a little bit of the language that almost all the students in the district speak. But when dealing with RAD, having any sort of high expectations will only lead to one disappointment after another. Que será, será, I suppose.

———

The educational system is creating generations of students that expect high marks in classes without the actual rigor that is supposed be to part of the class... and part of the debacle is that every department is bickering about what constitutes "rigor" so much, that we've forgotten that our various disciplines have become little more than a curiosity to most students, if at all an interest that might pull them from YouTube for a scant moment or two. The students will take that easy-A class in order to keep their GPA up and eventually get accepted to a four-year university because their transcripts are not a true reflection of what they did, or did not, do in high school. These are the students that will be the first to complain that their school did not properly prepare them for college when they end up taking remedial classes for at least their first year of post-secondary education.

Lisa: *I can't do this Bart, I'm not strong enough.*

Bart: *I thought you came here looking for a challenge.*

Lisa: *Duh... a challenge I could do.*

(The Simpsons)

These same students (as previously mentioned) that end up in remedial classes are the same ones who will complain on social media that they are learning the same things (which they obviously didn't the first time around) as they did in high school. The reason that they will be taking similar classes is because they did not score high enough on the placement exams to qualify for college level courses. It's an Ouroboros: a snake head eating its own tail. Students who have never demonstrated sufficient objective performance failing to demonstrate sufficient subjective performance, and thus remediated; requiring more courses before graduation. It's as tragic as it is convenient, at least for the university cash register.

It is this process of promotion that, regardless of learning, has created an ecosystem where mediocrity is glorified, and is the standard by which we now push students through to higher education. For those that do not choose to go to college, they leave high school and head off into the real-world to survive with little or no pragmatic skills; whereas those who do attend college, as I've mentioned many times, end up in one of the number of increasing remedial classes thanks to the auto-promote system that is now in place for many schools across the country.

This is the system that is currently in place, has been in place, and more than likely will be in place for many years to come. Those teachers who we've all worked with that are making it easy, and the administrators that are praising these teachers (along with that of the students for their high grades), are the ones doing a real disservice to the students; but that doesn't matter to them. In their eyes, grades are a reflection of learning, and as long as those students are somehow getting A's and B's in their classes regardless of what little learning, if any, is actually taking place, then RAD et al. will simply look at the grades and continue to praise both teacher and student for a job well done.

With more schools becoming dependent on technology as the years pass, it's not surprising that more glitches are starting to appear in the system. You can't really fault the students for taking advantage of these systemic glitches, as their awareness of the bugs comes from administration taking advantage of these same bugs in order to improve whatever data values they are trying to manipulate. It is these same administrators that will constantly harp on the importance of maintaining high standards in our classrooms and raising the bar of academic rigor... yet who are the very ones signing off on these last-minute moves to put students into online recovery classes in order to miraculously make-up their missing credits with less than a month left before graduation.

- 5 -

Acute Myopia

An issue that frequently comes up in discussions of education (especially on social media), be it about any level of schooling from kindergarten through college, is how few classes actually prepare students for the "real-world" once all of the schooling eventually is completed. The majority of comments are usually along the lines as to how education has morphed to more classes that focus on Shakespeare or the quadratic formula, and less that teach you how to file your own taxes or, as is the case of one comment from a college student that I read on twitter, marriage (there are some things that cannot be taught in the classroom).

There was a time when schools offered classes that allowed students who didn't feel they were college bound to learn an actual skill that they could take with them when they graduated from high school. This was also the time that college, though an option, was not pushed to be the only next step after twelve years of schooling (not to mention that it was a little more affordable than it is today).

"Behold: Waldorf education in action. Getting our hands dirty and learning by doing." – Lisa Simpson (The Simpsons)

The reason that many of these hand-on classes are disappearing and why they are no longer offered or replaced (which usually happens once the teacher of these classes retires), is because of the focus of the STEM (Science, Technology, Engineering, and Math) curriculum as well as standardized testing. This push for the focus of science and math has substantially reduced the variability of course offerings over the last few decades which, by the way, isn't exactly news to anyone.

Understand that I am not saying that STEM is a bad thing (and I know an 'A' for arts is occasionally added to create STEAM), but not every student across the country is interested in the same things as every other student, or their teachers for that matter. But it's this convergence and narrowing down of the types of classes being offered that is making it more difficult for both the student and the teacher. School curriculums should have more diversity of class offerings than they currently do. Most of the classes being taught are considered to be the core classes as they are the ones that focus on testing and are also the most looked at when students apply to go to college. This act of narrowing down the variety of classes so that a school can raise its test scores is really getting to the point of absurdity.

Consider for a moment the school that I currently work at that has about a ninety-five percent Hispanic population. Many of the students have Spanish listed on their file as being the main language spoken in the home. Now that we have that out of the way, go ahead and take a guess at the school's only foreign language offering. Go ahead, guess... I'll wait a minute. Think you figured it out? Yep, it's Spanish! The only foreign language that the school currently offers is the same language spoken in the majority of homes in the area. It's not a Chinese dialect, or Japanese, or even French that the school once offered;

it's Spanish. That's the school's current and only class for a student to fulfill their foreign language requirement... seriously!

Understanding that there is the argument that just because a person can speak a certain language doesn't mean that a person is able to read or write the language. This is absolutely correct, which is why the school also offers Spanish for Native Speakers. No, this isn't a joke or sarcasm, this is currently all there is to offer a student to fulfill their foreign language requirement.

Many schools are also losing classes outside of the core set that RAD simply does not consider to be of any value to a student. And when I say value, I mean it doesn't teach anything specifically that will be on the standardized test at the end of the year and offers nothing when it comes to the test scores of the school. But as I will be talking about shortly, it is not very difficult to take an elective class that RAD does not consider valuable when it comes to their obsession with test results, and to create a curriculum with those classes which could easily yield better test scores than just having classes that are geared towards learning something that might show up as a question on a test.

—

As the years progress, there simply seem to be less hands-on classes and more classes about theory as opposed to practice. Believe it or not, there was a time—albeit quite a few years ago—when both types of classes could co-exist within a school's master schedule. But once again, because of the stress of school image and the desire to keep up enrollment to keep the dollars coming in, administration has found that many of the hands-on classes simply do not offer what is needed to raise those test scores. As I mentioned back in the first chapter, it is this misunderstanding of how these types of classes could help to raise a school's performance as well as offering more variety for the students (not to mention teaching them something pragmatic) that is leading to their removal.

One argument that you will probably hear from administration in regards to removing classes that teach a skill is that they are rectifying the situation through the recent move that many districts are making with Project Based Learning (PBL). In short, districts are paying tens (if not hundreds) of thousands of dollars to a certain institute to come in and train all of the teachers on PBL. For the record, I have no problem with implementing projects in the classroom which I have done ever since I started teaching, but as usual, it is the administrative reaction (as with any new flavor of the month acronym) that PBL is going to shift the academic paradigm.

The problem with the implementation of what RAD expects when it comes to PBL is not actually the projects themselves. The issue is the expectation that these multi-week projects be included into an already full pacing plan that teachers are expected to follow which, as you'll see later on, is already a convoluted mess. The assumption that administration has is that somehow this interjection of more things to cover with the number of items that need to be covered, along with the amount of practice testing that they want teachers to do, add to that the number of days a teacher is pulled out of the classroom for some nonsensical reason thereby leaving the students with a substitute, as well as the number of days students will miss due to fieldtrips, rallies, leaving early for a sporting event, and any of the many other reasons that a student will miss class (let's not forget to add in sick days for both student and teacher), and well, you finally start to see the irrational expectations that administration has on teachers to get through what they are supposed to teach during a school year.

It is this press for PBL that is an excellent example of just of how myopic administration is when it comes to their vision of education. It's this attempt by RAD to get every teacher to utilize PBL in their classroom, all the while cutting actual classes from a school's master schedule that are project based and teach students an actual skill that are either gone, or are rapidly decreasing in number until they are also no longer part of a school's course of offerings.

The reduction of the number of class offerings is a direct relation to the emphasis on the end of year testing that schools seem to focus on more and more. This is not exactly anything new to anyone who pays attention to education in this country. But as I mentioned earlier, the trimming of these elective classes is not the fault of the standardized testing so much as it is the misunderstanding of how the classes that are being removed from the schedule can help students prepare for a post K–12 life that doesn't lead to college; and how these classes could also help to increase test scores that administrators are so obsessed with.

Principal Skinner: *So, what's the word down at One School Board Plaza?*

Superintendent Chalmers: *We're dropping the geography requirement. The children weren't testing well. It's proving to be an embarrassment.*

Principal Skinner: *Very good. Back to the three R's.*

Superintendent Chalmers: *Two R's... come October.*

(The Simpsons)

In fact, when a long-time teacher of an elective class, such as ceramics, that is not directly related to some standard (whether it be Common Core or some other standards that a school district sees only as an individual bullet point as opposed to the bigger picture) eventually retires, these classes are rarely replaced with another teacher for the same elective. What more than likely will end up happening is that the newly opened position is flown as an addition for one of the core subjects such as math, English, or social science, or simply not flown at all in order to save the district some money.

If you think about a ceramics class, there is plenty of geometry involved in creating the objects. In fact, every time the students create something, have them do some calculations that allow them to estimate the volume and the surface area. Or how about maximizing the volume using the minimum amount of clay (like those optimization problems students will do in a calculus class). It is really that easy to take a project in a ceramics class that the majority of administrators (and more than likely teachers, counselors, and students) see only as an elective to fill a graduation requirement, and add some geometry standards to it. It also wouldn't take away much time at all from working on the project. All of this could easily be done at the end of a project once whatever it is the students are working on is finished and count for a small portion of the overall grade.

There is also a very good chance that the objects the ceramics students are creating are not going to be these perfectly uniform rectangular prisms. Well, what class talks about finding the surface area and volume of both uniform and non-uniform objects? That would be geometry (and to a greater extent, calculus). You see how this could work?

Many of these classes that are being removed are also the ones that the students enjoy the most. These are the elective classes that many administrators do not see as beneficial when it comes to standardized testing because they do not understand how a specific standard that is suggested to be taught in a math class can be learned and understood to a higher degree in a ceramics class. This would give a ceramics teacher an opportunity to work with a math teacher to come up with a short post-project questionnaire that the students would complete after all is said and done. This would also be an example of a collaborative effort between two teachers of different curricula; which is one objective that every single principal that I have worked with has suggested that we as a staff need to accomplish. The idea of this type of project is one that RAD is always talking about, but never seems to understand how to make it happen.

Now let's take a look at an example of a topic from an auto-shop class: torque. Torque, if you aren't familiar with it, is a force multiplied by a radius or distance (the force and radius must be orthogonal (perpendicular) to each other). Just think of it as opening or closing a door. The farther you are from the hinge (which would represent the radius), the easier it is to open or close the door. The closer you are to the hinge, the more force is needed to open or close it. In other words, as the distance from the hinge increases, the amount of force needed to open or close the door decreases and vice-versa. This demonstrates that the values of force and radius are inversely related to each other when it comes to their product or torque.

In auto shop, students learn how to use a torque wrench. This is needed for pretty much every nut and bolt in a car or truck. That is to say that when a mechanic is working on an engine or replacing a tire, each bolt has a specific amount of torque as put forth by whatever company built the car. One does not, or shouldn't be, just tightening a bolt until it feels like it's nice and snug.

So then how does this auto-shop lesson tie-in with a lesson from algebra? For starters, not only does it connect with an algebra lesson, but it could also be related to a physics or engineering lesson. Since torque is the product of force and radius, then the teacher could easily have the students create a graphical representation of, just as an example, the amount of torque needed for a standard bolt for the wheel of a car which is (depending on the make and model) about eighty foot-pounds. The students could easily create a table of data for different values of force and radius. They could then plot these points on a force-radius diagram and will hopefully learn that the relationship is not linear. In fact, I went ahead and did that for you (for the example of the car and the eighty foot-pounds) just in case you were wondering.

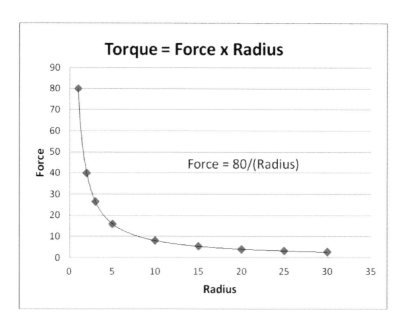

The story being told by the graph is pretty straight forward. If you have a torque wrench (feel free to google it) with a length of one foot, then you would need to apply eighty pounds of force to tighten the wheel bolt to dealer specifications. If the torque wrench were two feet in length, then you would only need to apply forty pounds of force and so on. And whether you are talking about an AP or Common Core standard, the ability to understand different types of numeric relationships along with the shape of their graph is pretty standards stuff. In the case of torque, the students would learn that an inverse relationship is hyperbolic as opposed to linear.

———

This was just one example of how something that was learned in an auto-shop class can be connected to multiple algebraic standards while at the same time teaching an applicable skill. Not to mention that it could easily be done during one class period, and also represents another example of cross-curricular learning. But don't hold your breath for an auto-shop class to reappear on a school's master schedule anytime soon, especially once it has been removed.

So unless this idea, or others like it, comes from someone in the small inner circle of people that run a school be they administrators or teachers, there is a very high probability that something like this will never happen. And if you do have a similar idea that you do propose to that small cohort in charge of your school, then you better make sure you send it through email or it is very likely that someone else will be taking credit for your idea.

The same goes for a drafting, woodshop, or home economics class (yes that's right, things learned in home-ec could easily be tied into standardized testing) and, since we are in the year 2018, a robotics class, a programming class, an Arduino class, a Raspberry Pi class, and so on. Many of these that I just mentioned are also connected to each other. An Arduino class could easily be tied into a robotics or even a drafting class. With so many things being automated today, even a wood-shop class could also be tied-in with Arduino and so on.

Here is a quick and dirty on the Arduino and Raspberry Pi, just in case you were wondering. Without getting into the nuances of either one, if you have ever checked the temperature of your house through your phone (or some other electronic device) and decided to turn on or off the air conditioning in your house using an app on your phone, then there is a pretty good chance that Arduino was involved. If you have ever used your phone to check the contents of your refrigerator remotely while you are at the supermarket (as many of these high-tech refrigerators are now able to do), then more than likely Raspberry Pi was involved.

So where are these classes today and why are they not being offered even more today than they were before they were removed in the early 2000s? The answer is pretty simple: Since the standards are always focused on the core classes, the people in charge of deciding whether or not these classes are needed do not see the tie-in to whatever the standards are that you are looking at, and therefore are not needed in a school's schedule of classes.

For those who want to fault Common Core or the College Board for removing these pragmatic classes, please understand—as I've mentioned before—that the onus of this action is not with the standards that are put forth, but the ignorance of those who are in charge of deciding what types of classes will best increase student performance on these exams.

Think of it this way, if I put every administrator at my district at a table and asked them what Raspberry Pi is, I can see one maybe two of them knowing that it has something to do with electronics and computers; and that's about as far as it would go. I can visualize some literally thinking that they were there to have some raspberry pie.

Lionel Hutz: *So Mr. Nahasapeemapetilon, if that is your real name, have you ever forgotten anything?*

Apu: *No. In fact I can recite pi to forty thousand places. The last digit is 1.*

Homer: *Mmm... pie.*

(The Simpsons)

About four years ago, I finally convinced the school to offer its first programming class ever: JavaScript. No, it's not the most powerful of languages, but it is a good introductory class for students who have never written a line of code in their lives. I had also been bringing this up and trying to get a programming class started since the early '00s. Let me stress this one more time: in the year 2013, I was finally able to get the school to offer its first computer programming class, ever. And even in the year 2018, there are still a number of schools that offer very little, if anything that has to do with computer science.

The principal at the time supported the idea and said that this class represented the future. My response was: "It was the future thirty years ago, now it's the present". But this is the mentality of the majority of people that are running school districts; they simply don't know. I'll go through the details of trying to get this class and others like it started in the chapter *Sisyphean Progress.*

These administrators simply do not understand how any of these hands-on classes that teach students a skill can be connected to a host of standards whether they are mathematical, language arts, or social science.

Let me talk a little more about the coding class and how it does relate to all three of those previously mentioned topics. I don't think people realize how much math and, in some cases, advanced math is used when writing a program. There is obviously basic algebra involved when it comes to some of the simpler calculations like where to put things on a screen, and if you are designing accounting software then you need to be able to keep track of the variables formulaically like you would do in any algebra class, or would have done in an accounting class.

If you take it one step further and you are working with some sort of animation, then the x-coordinate and y-coordinate are changing for every unit of time; differential equations anyone? Now if you are animating multiple items on a screen and they need to be able to change their direction if they collide (thereby creating a collision detection) with each other, then you are talking about the definition of continuity; calculus anyone?

But a programming class can easily include other curriculums as well. For my class, each student was required to write a two-to-three page research paper (I would have accepted more, but less was simply not acceptable), double spaced, each semester. I knew before even writing the course description that the class would not even be considered for the school's master schedule if it didn't contain a writing component to it.

The papers—which the students were informed about at the very beginning of the year—had to be about a person (first semester topic) or company (second semester topic) that has made (what the student writing the paper believed to be) a significant contribution to technology. The students had to include what they thought were the most important contributions that the person or company had on today's society. Part of the research paper had to take into consideration what world events at the time may have been the catalyst that perhaps drove the person or company to do whatever it was that they did. So even though it was a computer programming class, it also had aspects of writing and social science (albeit minimal, but it is better than not including them at all) that allowed for some cross-curricular assignments that are all the rage—well, at least one of them.

———

The list of classes that are being removed from a school's master schedule is rapidly shrinking because there are fewer and fewer classes that are left to be removed. As far as the few elective classes remaining are concerned, at some point they will be replaced by the small list of core classes until we get to the point where schools are only teaching a handful of subjects that have more to do with theory and very little, if any, with practice.

So what is it about those electives such as ceramics, the shoppe classes, accounting, and anything else that we have seen slowly disappearing from one school to another? As I've mentioned, they are simply not directly related to the end of the year testing and are therefore of no use to your revolving door administrator.

By bringing back these classes that rode off into the sunset sometime back in the late nineties to the early two thousands, students would be able to put theory into practice. Not to mention RAD would no longer have to hound the core subject teachers (with an already full curriculum to get through in a specific amount of time) as to why there isn't a month long project planned somewhere during the year, as there would be project based classes to go along with the standard core classes.

A student can learn more about geometry in a woodshop or drafting class than they ever could in a one year course of geometry studying nothing but theory with a compass and protractor (although both are rarely used anymore, especially the compass). Not to mention that the students taking these classes would also develop an understanding of how to take something that is learned from a book, or now more commonly a website, and apply it so as to make an ever important connection between theory and practice.

———

There are so many holes when being taught mathematics throughout the years that many students get more confused because something that they learned in one class is contradicted in another. The point is, that it's this misunderstanding of these classes from the revolving door administration that are leading to the demise of classes that could easily be used to teach specific mathematical ideas in an implicit form, and also help to fill in those gaps that if left unfilled, will only exacerbate the problems that the students are already having with the subject.

Many schools are constantly talking about bringing in many of these hands-on classes that I have mentioned earlier but not until the school is ready for it. Earlier, I mentioned Raspberry Pi and Arduino, and although administration, both site and district office, talk about bringing these types of classes (they don't actually know them by name and will usually just use the word "technology") to the school, I can honestly tell you that there is no way the site I work at will be offering any of these classes until at least the 2021–2022 school year; and that is being optimistic. I'll talk about how I got to that number in the next chapter.

What is amazing is the frequency that administration talks about the need to offer these types of classes and how we as a school system need to prepare our students for the future, and yet, they have no idea how to implement these classes into a school's schedule but will continue to pay lip-service when it comes to talking about the importance of incorporating these classes in the future. What they fail to see (yes again, but that shouldn't be surprising to anyone at this point) is that by the time we implement these 21st century classes into the school, they will already be an anachronism. And even if and when they do figure it out, the first thing administration will do is to spend thousands of dollars to attend a conference on whatever it is they want to implement. Sure they could just ask around or do a little research on their own to save some money, but that is not how education works.

In other words, administration seems to think that by going slower than the rest of the world, or other schools that are up to date on teaching 21st century skills, that we are somehow helping the students prepare for a post-secondary life.

"Let me get this straight, we're behind the rest of our class and we're going to catch-up to them by going slower than they are? Cuckoo." – Bart Simpson (The Simpsons)

So why not just bring these hands-on classes back or, better yet, replace them with their modern day equivalents? Since the majority of schools offered these skill-based classes in the past, then would it really be so difficult to bring them back and update them to reflect that of a modern day environment?

The obvious answer would be a *no*, it would not be difficult to bring them back, but doing so is not the biggest issue.

The main problem is that many of these classes would require someone to come in and teach them that have the expertise in one of the areas that I previously mentioned. But how many people that are experts in Arduino, Raspberry Pi, or the bladeless turbine engine (Tesla) would be interested in teaching at a local high school for at least a fifty percent cut in pay, and taking on a class of thirty-plus students of which maybe ten would be interested in learning about the craft? And even if they did decide to do this for whatever reasons, they would still have to deal with and be evaluated by administrators that would have no idea what they are talking about when it comes to what they are teaching in the classroom. And yet, if this person who is an expert in their field and did decide to teach at a local high school, but for some reason did not get along with his or her evaluator, then it is more than likely this person would receive a poor evaluation and will probably be out of a job long before tenure kicks in.

On top of being paid less and dealing with large class sizes (not to mention having to deal with you know who), the people that are the experts in these fields would also need a valid teaching credential just to be able to teach, regardless of whatever their field of study may be.

One side note about these elective classes, as I mentioned a couple of paragraphs ago, is that maybe ten of thirty-plus students would be interested in learning the craft which makes things even more difficult for the teacher. One thing you might not know (if you aren't a teacher) is that elective classes are usually referred to as a "dumping ground" for students. Very often, a student who has a six-period day will have a hole or two in their schedule at the beginning of the school year; so the counselor of the student will usually fill that gap with an elective class. If there is a class available that the student prefers and there is an open seat, then the student will be enrolled into that class. But if the class they want is full and there are no other sections available, then the student will be put into a different elective class regardless as to whether or not they are interested in the subject. So if the school did somehow find an Arduino expert who was willing to take a pay-cut and work with a full class, it is because of this need to fill in the holes of a student's schedule that will result in a class where many of the students are simply not interested.

So let's pretend for a moment that some engineer saw a position for an electronics or physics teacher at a local high school at a revolving-door district. Maybe he or she wants to take a hiatus from the world of engineering and teach their skill at one of the local schools. They create an edjoin.org account and start uploading files to their profile by adding a résumé, some letters of recommendation, a letter of introduction, and some references. But they would soon find out that they would not be able to apply for any of the jobs posted online because they were missing a couple of items.

The first item would be a teaching credential. How many people that are already experts in their fields would want to spend at least a year (not to mention the money) sitting through some classes to obtain a teaching credential in order to get a job that would amount to a fifty percent (more than likely way more than that, especially since they will be a first-year teacher) cut in pay?

The would-be teacher would then realize that they are missing another part of getting a teaching job, which would be proof of their subject-matter competency. There are a couple of ways, at least in the state of California, that this could be achieved. The first step would be to take a few classes in the field (it is possible that they might be able to have them waived because they took similar classes to earn their degree) that they want to teach even though they are already an expert in their field. And though they are more qualified to teach the classes themselves than some other teacher with no experience in the same field, they still need to take and pass these classes in order to show competence in the subject that they want to teach.

The second step is to pass at least two standardized tests (they are far from free). Those would be the California Basic Educational Skills Test (CBEST) and at the very least, the California Subject Examination for Teachers (CSET).

So once this engineer takes a year to get their teaching credential and passes at least those two exams (there are probably more, but we'll just stick with those two for now), they are then ready to take that pay-cut, have a class of thirty-plus students, and be evaluated by someone that has no experience in the engineering field, nor will understand anything that is being taught.

Now there is that whole argument that it's completely possible that this engineer, as intelligent as he or she may be, might not be someone that is suited for the teaching profession—which is a valid point. But then how many physics teachers (just as an example, as this could be any subject; so don't get upset if you are a physics teacher) have there been who had no experience in the world of physics, and got the job just because they had a supplementary teaching credential in the physics field and passed one or two competency exams? Many of these teachers also do not have a degree in the field of science, but what they do have over the engineer is the right paperwork, and perhaps even better interviewing skills than that of our would-be engineering teacher. And if the interview does not go very well for the engineer (even though they are more than qualified for the job when it comes to knowing the material) the person that will be selected to teach engineering to the students would most likely be the one with little or no experience in that field to begin with.

In the end, the person who gets the job may just be the one

that has very little, if any, idea on how to teach the subject along with a limited understanding of the topics that encompass the class. Not to mention that if one of the interviewees is a good friend with some administrator in the district, it is very likely— regardless of how qualified or unqualified this person may be— that the friend of the administrator will get the job over the person with the actual understanding of the subject.

This example is just one reason why schools are hurting for teachers when it comes to teaching specific math and science courses. There has been some talk about giving people that have worked in specialized fields a "pass" when it comes to some of the credential classes and proving subject matter competence, but this talk has also been going on since I started teaching back in 1999; so don't hold your breath for some type of resolution for the issue to happen anytime soon.

If you aren't in education, then you might be somewhat dismayed as to how many teachers do not have a degree (or just a strong background for that matter) in the subject that they teach; this is especially true in the math and sciences. Granted, that it is not necessary for a person to have a great understanding of a subject who does not have a degree in said subject to teach it successfully, but it really does help.

Math Teacher 1: *How much was one percent in Roman days?*

Math Teacher 2: *Try ask.com.*

Two math teachers during a project based learning meeting... *seriously*! Let me say that one more time... *seriously*!

Now suppose you are a teacher and took these ideas about adding classes like the ones just mentioned (or bringing back the old classes with a modern day spin) and why they should be brought back to your site administrator. Now take it one step further and suppose you explained how resurrecting the old shop classes, home-ec, or accounting, and also explained how these classes would also assist in raising the school's test scores on any sort of end-of-course exam; all the while teaching the students something that they could easily put to good use once they get out of high school.

As a teacher, you could take these ideas and explain to your site or district office administrator and not only show them how to implement these classes back into a school's master schedule, but also show evidence as to how this will help with their obsession of standardized testing; but if you did take the time and effort to do so, do not expect any reciprocation of your enthusiasm from RAD. You could do all of this and then some, and still be staring down the vapid-viscous void of someone who has no idea what it is you are talking about, nor the foresight to understand how this type of actual innovation (as opposed to taking something that another school district is doing and implementing regardless as to whether or not it will work, and considering that to be innovative) in the classroom would help to best prepare students for the jobs of today and tomorrow.

In fact, you could probably take a cure for cancer to RAD (of course you would never do that because it would go nowhere with them) and offer to teach it in a class that doesn't exist in the master schedule, and they would come up with some excuse as to why it wouldn't work well with the current schedule, but that it might be possible to add it in a year or two.

"You know what I am? I'm a dog chasing cars. I wouldn't know what to do with one if I caught it." – The Joker (The Dark Knight, 2008)

So for those of you reading that have wondered why and where these classes are disappearing to, or why modern day hands-on classes are not being brought into the curriculum for many schools, you need look no further than the inept, shortsighted, *I wouldn't know what to do with it if it fell into my lap*, RAD. It should also not be very surprising that as much stress as Nouveau Administration puts on a 21st century classroom, they certainly don't seem to be in much of a hurry when it comes to incorporating a 21st century curriculum.

- 6 -

Sisyphean Progress

Hopefully, you are now able to realize how unresponsive site or district administration is to change (at least when the change is proposed by a non-inner-circle teacher) when it comes to updating our current curriculum to something a little more related to the 21st century classroom on which they seem to put so much emphasis.

As much as RAD touts the importance of change and how being static when it comes to education is not exactly progressive, they certainly don't seem to be in too much of a hurry to make these changes that they are always talking about.

"There's a lot of f#ck!n' hard talk around here and not a lot of follow through." – Derek Vinyard (American History X, 1998)

The following are two examples of issues that schools similar to mine have had for many years. The first example is based around the effort of getting classes into a school's schedule that are geared toward learning a skill that allows a student to begin their career before getting out of high school. The second example has to do with a long-standing problem that has plagued not only my school, but numerous others as well; which is the issue of the number of eighth-grade students who arrive at the high school as incoming freshmen who only understand mathematics at the fourth or fifth-grade level—and some even less.

For the first example, let me explain how I came up with the year 2022 (from the previous chapter) before our district would see its first computer engineering class such as Arduino or Raspberry Pi, or any class that has to do with engineering and computers for that matter.

After about thirteen years of trying, I was finally able to get the school's first programming class on the schedule in the year 2013. The class is simply an introduction to HTML and JavaScript with the focus being on writing code in JavaScript. The students did some small projects ranging from a basic image slide-show to creating their own version of pong. The variability of the projects was enough to introduce them to the basic commands that are present across the majority of programming languages. Though it was just an intro class, there's enough content such that if they wanted to branch out and learn other coding languages, then at least they would have a good idea on how to get started.

Let me backtrack for just a moment as to how I was even able to get the school's first coding class on the schedule to begin with after trying for so many years. About half way through the 2012 school year—after the November election in which the community voted to oust all but one board member—the new board members decided to bring in a new principal who served as a vice principal at my site a few years back. It was the new principal's job to clean up the giant mess (it's not possible for me to stress how much of a mess was left behind) as well as to fix the toxic and dystopian environment that the previous principal and board had created.

I pitched the idea of the coding class when he first arrived and pointed out how nothing had changed since he was here last, and that something needs to be done at this district to start teaching the students something a little more pragmatic than just some theory to do well on standardized testing. He agreed and was able to help me get the class on the schedule for the next school year.

The problem was that after four years of teaching the class, there was still only one section and it usually consists of juniors and seniors who had never written a line of code in their lives. The issue with just having juniors and seniors in the class is that there will never be a more advanced class on site unless the students start arriving at the high school having had some exposure to computer programming. But as I will talk about at the end of the chapter, a more advanced class (at least at this school) will most likely also never happen.

After two years of teaching the class, I suggested to the principal (the same one, believe it or not, that helped me to get the class started, but whose attitude had gone from that of a hard working principal to that of one who does nothing but delegates responsibilities) that perhaps a simpler version of the class could be offered at the middle schools in order to eventually have a more advanced class or even start an AP (Advanced Placement) Java class.

So when I pitched the idea of me going one period a day to one of the middle schools, I thought he would be all for it, which he was at least to some degree, and did show some support and a little bit of enthusiasm for the idea. The problem was—as it always is in education—when it came down to cost. If I were to teach a class at the middle school, then there would be one section of math that I wouldn't be teaching at the high school, and because this class wasn't for his site, then it might have hurt the site's budget by having to pay someone else to teach the one class that I wouldn't be on campus to do. This is when the aforementioned enthusiasm quickly waned, and he had no interest in pitching this idea to the principal of the middle school or the superintendent.

——

Another year passed and I decided to try again. This time a couple of the vice principals were in the office with the principal and I pretty much pitched the same idea. I explained how teaching this class at the middle schools would eventually lead to a more advanced class and possibly an AP Java class down the road and, once again, teach a pragmatic skill as well as helping the students understand how mathematics ties in with computer programming. All three of the administrators really liked the idea and, for yet another year, that is where the idea came to an end; praised and left clipped to the refrigerator like a high test score or a song that Ringo wrote for the Beatles (that was a *Family Guy* reference by the way—bonus points for looking it up).

So this year, I decided to just go over site administration's head and go straight to the Assistant Superintendent in Charge of Curriculum and pitch the idea to that person. Understand that the current person in that position was just literally put into that position the day before I went in to talk about the idea.

As luck would have it, the new person in this position was not able to meet with me because they were just appointed to the position (a decision made at the June board meeting when the deck of administrators was shuffled and many received a promotion) at the board meeting that had just taken place the previous night. So the person that I thought I was going to talk to (who held the position for less than two years) was replaced with someone else who had no experience with that position.

And even though I knew the outcome even before I tried to setup an appointment, I still decided to try and meet with this person. It was then recommended by the secretary (as when I went to visit this person at the district office, all of the new appointees were in a meeting) that I send an email out to this person and make an appointment to discuss what would be the intentions of the meeting. Understand that this was less than one week after the school year ended and the board was already making changes in site and district office administration.

Now it's important to understand that my rationale for trying to have this meeting so quickly after the recent school year had ended was in hopes to get an introductory class going at one of the middle schools for the next year. Since it was still early June, it would not have been much of an issue to include the class in the upcoming academic year, or so I thought.

I sent out an email essentially saying the same things that I pitched to my site administrators, and the response was pretty much the same—with the exception that this person was willing to talk about making it happen... but wasn't available to meet until sometime in late July as she was leaving on vacation the next day. In other words, instead of offering an introductory programming class at a middle school for the 2017–2018 school year, it wouldn't be until at least the 2018–2019 school year before even laying the groundwork.

Here is the response that I received from this person a few weeks before the next school year began explaining to me what I needed to do in order to make this happen were all of the things I had already done. But at the same time, I really wasn't surprised at the response.

As I inquired about your request a little further, the process would need to begin with your site administrator and the administrators of the middle schools. Master Schedule is site based and determined by people at the site. Additionally, please work with [insert principal name here]—this idea would need the approval of your site administrator as it would impact the Master Schedule as well. – RAD

And this is how, after having first tried to implement the idea in 2016–2017, I arrived at the calculation of the 2021–2022 school year before any Arduino or Raspberry Pi class is even offered (I'm not holding my breath that they will be though). Practically speaking, in order to work with either of those fairly common pieces of equipment, a person needs to understand the basics of coding, and without at least an introductory course, it will be a little more difficult for someone to pick up on how to work either one, so time is of the essence— which is exactly why it's such a good example of why the speed of actual change in curriculum (despite the strong talk and conviction) is, at best, glacial.

Suppose the 2018–2019 school year was the first middle school class to learn the basics of programming and also suppose that this is an 8th grade class. With school boards and administration being the way they are, they will more than likely want at least one year of the class before even considering offering the next level. In other words, the 2019-2020 year is simply out of the question. So the first academic year that they might take into consideration adding something new would be for the 2020–2021 school year. But this will only happen if someone at the top talks to someone else at the top of another school district that is doing something similar. They will then bring the idea in as their own and talk about how progressive these types of classes can be for the students. Knowing what I know about this district, I would honestly put an implementation date for any classes like these sometimes around the year 2025. No, that isn't sarcasm and yes, that is still being very optimistic.

Making this even worse and even more hypocritical is the fact that these classes are project based. Administration has been adamant more than ever about incorporating project based learning (PBL) into the classroom. And yet, when you give them something that is not only project based, but also up to date when it comes to teaching something that has to do with present day technology, they simply will not budge on it until they are given a directive from someone at the top or, if they are the top as I mentioned, get the idea from some other person at the top of some other district where they have not only implemented these types of classes, but have also had success in doing so.

On top of that, classes like these help with understanding mathematics (lots of group and set theory when it comes to coding as well as some application of differential equations), critical thinking, problem solving, and all of those other skills that RAD continues to ask teachers to include in their lessons. And even though there are teachers out there pushing for classes like these to be added to what a school offers, there just is simply no way it will happen unless it comes from a board member, the superintendent, or one of the cronies of the inner circle. And the way these people find out about classes like this is usually by reading about some other school that has already tried it and, as I mentioned, also had success with it, or spent three days at a conference where they attended a one hour presentation on the subject. But what they won't do is bother taking a look as to whether or not the school district that they are now in control of has what is needed to do what other schools have already done. In other words, the automatic assumption is that if it worked for some other school, then it will also work for ours; but not until then.

"Don't you sometimes wonder if it's worth all this? I mean what you're fighting for." – Rick Blaine (Casablanca, 1946)

This entire process of trying to either start a new class, or (as in the previous example) take an existing class and offer it at a different school in order to expose students to the world of computer programming can only be described as Sisyphean. The fact that many administrators will not even give something like this a second thought unless the thought comes from within their circle of cronies, only goes to show how obtuse RAD is when it comes to making actual changes. Then again, implementation doesn't really matter to RAD. All that matters is that they talk about bringing in these types of classes to show that they are being progressive in front of the right people in order to demonstrate that they are earning their pay, and that there is a need for their position.

—

And now for boulder number two (no, I still haven't learned my lesson). This situation is about the number of students arriving at the high school who are unprepared for high school math. For those of you teaching post K–12 (be it a college or a tech school) understand that you are not the only ones getting students that are unprepared. We're doing all we can to get them to middle school level of understanding before they graduate, and even that is a challenge.

The thing is that everyone knows that this is a problem. From the middle school principal and teachers, to their high school counterparts, to the superintendent of the school district, to the local school board, to the Chair at any college, anywhere. In other words, we all know this issue exists, we talk about it, pen a solution on a piece of paper, and as usual, that is where it comes to an end. And every now and then a dumbass like me comes up with a pretty simple solution to the problem only to have it go nowhere because it didn't come from a six-figure person over at the nicely temperature-regulated district office.

The solution was pretty simple, but nothing really new: give the incoming ninth-grade students a diagnostic test. I know that's some outside-of-the-box thinking there now isn't it? But that was only part of the solution. I'm just emphasizing it to show how little administration pays attention to someone that isn't in their inner circle (especially a person who is every vocal against many of their misguided ideas that they got from some other school or some inspirational YouTube video). After all, giving a diagnostic test isn't really anything new.

So I came up with a test that had some basic topics that were no higher than what is expected of a fifth-grade math student. You'll see some of the questions in a moment, but before looking at the questions that were given to ninth and tenth-grade algebra students, it is important to understand that the questions were not graded as simply right or wrong. Partial credit was given based on a rubric. So if a student did the majority of a division problem correctly, but just got the remainder wrong for whatever reason, then they still received most of the credit.

The test was written with four questions for a specific standard with the focus being on addition, subtraction, multiplication, and division. The first problem of the four being the easiest, the two middle problems being of mid-level difficulty, and a fourth problem that would be considered as a little more of a challenge... for a fourth or fifth-grade student.

What follows are some questions exactly as they appeared on the diagnostic; the percentage of students that received full credit for the problem; the grade level of the standard, and the level of difficulty for each problem. No calculator was allowed, just in case you were wondering. But as you saw in my last book (if you read it) a high school student using a calculator on a middle school exam doesn't necessarily imply they will get the correct answer.

Question 3: $\begin{array}{r} 5{,}384 \\ +\,2{,}176 \\ \hline \end{array}$ 85%   Grade 3   Mid

Question 6: $\begin{array}{r} 465 \\ -\,179 \\ \hline \end{array}$ 85%   Grade 3   Mid

Question 8: $\begin{array}{r} 5{,}274 \\ -\,984 \\ \hline \end{array}$ 65%   Grade 3   High

Question 9: $\begin{array}{r} 37 \\ \times\,10 \\ \hline \end{array}$ 67%   Grade 4   Low

Question 12: $\begin{array}{r} 581 \\ \times\,72 \\ \hline \end{array}$ 61%   Grade 4   High

Question 14: $3\overline{)247}$ 40%   Grade 4   Mid

Question 16: $43\overline{)13{,}245}$ 10%   Grade 5   High

Question 17: $\dfrac{1}{3} + \dfrac{2}{5}$ 41%   Grade 5   Mid

Question 18: $\dfrac{7}{8} - \dfrac{3}{4}$ 41%   Grade 5   Mid

The reason I wrote it this way instead of giving some online diagnostic exam on basic pre-algebra such as the topic of slope or solving two-step equations, was that it is much easier for a math teacher to find the gaps in a student's understanding through basic number sense questions than it is from a multiple choice test where there is a twenty-five percent chance of guessing an answer correctly. This test took a long time for the teachers to grade, but really gave us a good insight to where the issues are when it comes to a student's understanding of basic arithmetic. And if you have been teaching math long enough, you know that things usually fall apart for students around the fourth grade when they start learning about parts of numbers as opposed to only dealing with whole numbers.

Here are the overall results from the students that took the exam.

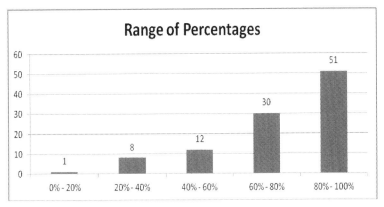

Based on these results, we came to the conclusion that at least twenty-one students needed some sort of extra help to get up to par with the rest of the class. Now some of the teachers felt that the third-grade set of questions were a little too easy, so I ran the numbers with only the results of the fourth and fifth-grade concepts. So if you narrowed it down to just the fourth and fifth-grade topics, then you can see in the graph that follows that at least thirty-eight students that were, and more than likely still are, in need of extra help.

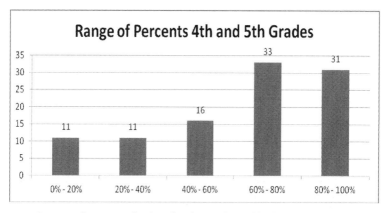

Some of you might be thinking that all of the students that were not in the 80%–100% range should have been identified as a student that was in need of assistance and you would be correct, but it would have been nice just to get those who scored sixty percent or less to have attended the after school tutoring that was set up for students who needed extra help. I'll get back to that in a little bit.

"If something needs to happen with this sh!t, it needs to happen now!" – Jimmy Smith Jr. (8 Mile, 2002)

The results and test were then shown (there were pages of graphs—not just the ones shown—that also looked at the results of each of the individual questions) to the principal of the school and vice principal in charge of curriculum. They were appalled at the results (as they should have been) and agreed something should be done get these students up to grade level. Being that I have been in the system for so long, I knew that when they said something should be done, it really meant that I should be the person to get that something done; so I continued.

Next, I was able to find a counselor that was willing to work with me by meeting with the students and helping to make contact with the parents of the students that underperformed on the exam. The last part was to find a place to do this and anyone that would be willing to help tutor the students after school. The good news was that there was, and still is, an after school program that was on site thanks to a grant for just this type of situation. They had many tutors that were there after school, and they were willing to contact all of the parents on the list that we gave to them. So not only were the parents hearing from a counselor and a teacher, they were also hearing from this after school program.

I know, it sounds like this is all going to work out well, but alas, it didn't. But before getting into why (feel free to take a guess) it failed, let's take a look at what we have so far.

For starters, we had students whose basic number skills were identified to be at, or less than, the fourth and fifth-grade levels—but yet were expected to perform well at a ninth-grade curriculum. And for emphasis, this has been an ongoing issue at this school, and many others, for years.

Next, we have administrative acknowledgement that there is a problem and they were given plenty of data to show how bad the problem really is. Understand that they did not need the data to know this was happening, but it did give them some more insight as to magnitude of the problem. And as data hungry as administration is, it seems as if the data simply does not matter unless it is regarding an issue that matters to them; which is just a nice way of saying that it doesn't matter to them until the some administrator over at the district office tells them that a specific problem is suddenly needs to matter to them.

Finally, we had parental contact from the teachers, a counselor, and an after school program specifically there to help students in need of extra help for whatever classes they were struggling in.

So take a guess at who made no phone calls (even though they are constantly stressing the importance of making phone calls, but I guess that is just meant for teachers and counselors), didn't talk to any of the students, or even brought up the subject after the initial discussion? You guessed it: the one and only RAD. The only support from RAD was verbally when I originally proposed the idea. No questions regarding making a few phone calls or meeting with parents and students to help get the program underway. This wasn't exactly surprising to me (or any of you reading this who are, or are not, in education) as this is just the nature of working in the field. But even without their assistance, we were still able to do what was needed to get the after-school program started. And even though those of us that put the program together had high hopes for the end result, we were also realistic and knew that a high turnout was not very probable.

In the end, once everything was up and running, a total of five students showed up... but not all on the same day. Within two weeks none of the five were showing up anymore regardless of parental contact.

When the teachers of the students asked them why they stopped going or simply didn't show up to begin with, the answer was pretty much the same: "*Why should I go when I'm not getting credit for it?*" The students simply did not care that going after school would help them fill in the gaps going all the way back to fifth-grade or even earlier. They know that they can go to summer school which is usually an easy passing grade as the summer school teacher usually just does whatever he or she feels like doing, and does not really have to follow the guidelines of the standard curriculum. And since the school has a ninety-seven percent graduation rate, the students are fully aware as to how little they can do for each class and still have no problem graduating.

"Oh, good grief." - Charlie Brown

———

At an inner-city, low-performing school, many parents do not respond to teacher or counselor phone calls. Many teachers, counselors, and even RAD have been hung up on while trying to contact a parent or guardian. They especially don't respond to after school programs that really have no effect on whether or not their son or daughter will graduate. Unless they are called into a meeting with a teacher and a vice principal or, better yet, the principal, they simply see the situation from the same perspective of the student.

But the attitude of why bother attending if they are not getting credit for doing so shouldn't be a surprise to anyone; especially by the time that these students have reached high school. They already passed all of the grades leading up to high school, so why should they have to go to tutoring after school to do the same things that they were already promoted for understanding as indicated by the passing grades they, or did not, receive? And even though the data is there to prove that they don't understand what they should have learned, they simply will not go unless they get some sort of reward for attending.

And now for the best part: Fast-forward to the first department meeting of the new school year, where the foci and central topics are brought up and discussed. The big discussion question from administration was basically this: *What could we as a school do to bridge the gap for the students that struggled in middle school to be successful at the high school?* It's a good thing it wasn't the English department, or else they may have collapsed from exhaustion at trying to explore that amount of irony.

Here we were at the beginning of the next school year, and starting all over again with the debate as to how we can fix this never-ending problem. It was as if the entire attempt that was put forth just a few months back suddenly never happened. One other teacher in the meeting brought it up in the form of a whisper: *"Didn't you try to do something last year about this problem?"* I just kind of nodded my head and just pretended to listen to whatever it was RAD was saying at the time. Yes, it's possible that it could have worked, but I guess I'll leave that part for the scholars to figure out.

"What-If is a game for scholars." – Philip II (The Lion In Winter, 1968)

So for those of you wondering how a teacher eventually reaches the *Capitulation* (see chapter 11) phase of their career, these were just two examples of how RAD is simply not interested in solutions to problems unless those solutions are dictated from someone above, whom they can then compliment on how good of an idea it is. I can assure you that if the superintendent called the principal and told him to do the exact same thing that I attempted, the program would be in full swing.

Now when it comes to something like the after-school tutoring program that isn't part of the official school schedule, it was possible to get it started without the assistance of administration. But as you read, without some sort of teeth, these programs will simply never get off the ground. But when it comes to getting new classes on the schedule or, as in my case, trying to get a similar class that is currently taught at the high school to also be offered at the middle school, there is simply no way to make that happen without administration signing off on it and the board of education approving it.

There just comes that point after pushing the boulder up the hill only to have it roll all the way back down (in many cases farther from the base of the hill than it originally started) so many times, that many teachers simply decide that it's just not worth trying to push anymore. Sometimes it's easier to just show up, teach the classes you were assigned, and just go with the routine. So then, have I finally learned my lesson? Of course I haven't. But it is getting a little tougher to push that boulder up the hill as the years continue to pass.

Ralph: *Daddy, how come you're not at work?*

Clancy: *I don't know. How come you're not at school?*

Ralph: *My teacher says she's tired of trying.*

(The Simpsons)

———

But now let's go back for a moment to boulder number one and talk about why a more advanced coding class will probably never happen and the 2025 date is also pretty much out of the cards.

After four years of teaching the introduction to coding class that took me thirteen years to get started, it will not be offered for the 2018–2019 school year. The reason for this is simple: money... again. Because the class only averages 18 students per year (which worked out nicely because I only had 19 functioning laptops), and because of recent decisions made by the administrative powers over at the district office of cutting one math teaching position and one English teaching position, there is simply no room for a math teacher to have a class of only 18 when I can be teaching a class of Algebra 1 freshmen that will be packed to the contractual upper limit of thirty-six students.

So after pushing the boulder up for the last four years—

seventeen if you take into consideration that I've been trying to get this class started since my second year of teaching—to get the programming class started, and also trying to make progress with respect to offering more classes that are related to computer programming and eventually engineering, the boulder has rolled back down from whence I originally started to push... and decided to stop right on my toes.

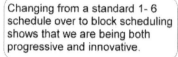

- 7 -

Remedial Classes and Matchboxes

I've written quite a bit about how schools within districts are lowering the bar when it comes to course content in order to keep their promotion rates, or in the case of high schools their graduation rates, as high as they can possibly get them to go. But what I haven't talked much about is the domino effect that is created starting from the elementary schools and carries all the way through, for those that make it, to college. And just in case you were wondering, the schools not lowering the bar are also those that do not have the same enrollment issues that might endanger an administrative position.

I know that I have mentioned jumping over matchboxes before, but just in case some of you aren't familiar with it, let me very briefly explain the reference. In the late sixties to early seventies (a little before my time... barely), there was a show called Monty Python's Flying Circus. As a side note and really nothing to do with the rest of the book at all, Monty Python and the Holy Grail is an absolutely awesome movie. I probably should have done what so many people suggested to me when I started teaching which was to *run away*! But then I would also not be penning the inner workings of many a school district across America; so I guess it does relate to this after all.

The matchbox reference has to do with a skit called: *The Upper-Class Twit of the Year* which is also sometimes referred to as *The Twit Olympics.* In this sketch (feel free to YouTube it), the competitors have to traverse through a series of daunting obstacles. Some of these obstacles are: Walking Along The Straight Line; Insulting The Waiter, and The Matchbox Jump. The last one has the contestants jumping over matchboxes stacked up on top each other. It is not as easy as it sounds as there is not one, but actually two matchboxes (depending on which version of *The Twit Olympics* that you watch) stacked on top of each other that each contestant needs to jump over to get to the next event. And although that may sound easy to you, not every competitor was able to get over the wall of matchboxes in the same fashion that many students are unable to get over a lowered bar regardless of how low that bar goes.

The part about all of this that seems to be somewhat of a quandary, to say the least, is that everyone knows that this is happening. Worse yet, is that no one really seems to be in any hurry to do anything about it. And not only are they [meaning those in charge of the school district] not doing anything about, but the rate at which the bar is falling is increasing which, if you think about it, makes sense from a physics standpoint as the force of gravity is inversely proportional to the square of the radius or height.

There are plenty of examples out there when it comes to what changes to curriculum that schools and districts are making in order to keep graduation rates up, and to also decrease the number D's and F's that students are getting in their classes.

A pretty basic example of the bar being lowered would be a

standard Algebra 1 class. The number of topics being taught in a typical Algebra 1 class is slowly decreasing year after year. If you had this class back in the '90s or early '00s (or before that) you would probably be somewhat dismayed not only how much less of a book is covered in the course of a school year, but also that it has slowly morphed into what a pre-algebra class was during those years.

As a side note, I know that there is this ongoing debate as to whether or not all students should be taking algebra in high school and that perhaps different tracks of mathematics should be available for students. You've probably figured out what my stance on this would be, but that isn't what I'm trying to get at right now. I will, however, be taking on this issue in a book down the road.

Each subsequent level of mathematics is also following the path of the Algebra 1 class. A standard class of Algebra 2 that is taught in many schools today is not much more than what was once considered to be the curriculum of an Algebra 1 class. A Pre-Calculus class today is no more than an Algebra 2 class used to be. In fact, a well taught Algebra 2 Honors class easily covers all that is taught in a general Pre-Calculus class.

Lois: *That's right Peter they [fire trucks] are red.*

Brian: *Uh Lois, what are you doing?*

Lois: *I switched Peter's questions to the preschool edition just to let him have his moment.*

(Family Guy)

One thing that is important to note, is that the algebra books today are pretty similar to those used in the classroom in the '90s (which were probably books that were purchased in the '80s) in regards to the number of ideas and chapters that are covered in one academic year. One nice thing about the newer books is that it requires less of an imagination when it comes to being able to visualize certain algebraic shapes as the graphics in the books today give a much clearer picture than the ones from twenty or thirty years ago. Yes, the odd answers are still in the back of the book, but that doesn't really matter anymore with websites such as Chegg and the rest of the internet. Teacher's solution manuals are not exactly difficult to find either. In fact, just in case you might not know this, there are plenty of apps out there that students can install on their phone, use it to take a picture of a problem, and have it generate an answer pretty much immediately, along with the steps to solve the problems.

And since we are on the topic, as a teacher myself I am actually ok with students finding answers to the problems that I assign. I usually give them the answers to show that I am more concerned with their logic and how they come up with a solution than that of just finding an answer to a question. One thing that I do find somewhat comical is how the students themselves don't seem to know that teachers are familiar with these websites or apps. Every time I show one of my classes the wolframalpha website (along with other websites and apps) and how it can be used to help them out, I usually get a response along the lines such as, "*You know about that?*" Although you might be surprised as to how many teachers do not know about websites like wolframalpha or how easy it is when it comes to finding the solutions to a particular textbook.

———

So let's take a look as to why the bar continues to get lower year after year until at some point it will be no higher than one matchbox and students will still not be able to get over it. The reasoning for this is quite simple and it goes along with what I wrote about in the previous chapter. Many students are coming up to the high-school level unprepared in a similar fashion that many students who graduate from high school and go to college end up taking remedial classes.

Many high schools have a pretty standard offering of math classes starting with Algebra 1 and finishing at the top with some AP Calculus or AP Statistics class. Obviously this traditional type of pathway isn't always suited for every student. There are schools that also offer a general statistics class and usually something for seniors that will be masked under the guise of "Business Math" or something along those lines. The reality is that it is usually just a fourth or fifth-grade level math class used to make sure that those seniors who do not have all of their math credits in order to graduate have a way to ~~earn~~ get them. And if they end up failing these fourth or fifth grade equivalent classes, then there is always that last-second online credit-recovery class to help get them to the procession.

What usually ends up happening is that many of the students that have a questionable mathematical background end up taking Algebra 1 their first year of high school. And since they have a weak background, they end up failing the class their freshman, and sometimes again, their sophomore year. The result is that more students have D's and F's on their transcripts than administration would like to see. The high number of bad grades then catches the eye of administration that leads them to start worrying about the graduation rate. We can't let that rate go down now, can we? Not to mention that students with D's and F's might not be able to get into the university that they choose once they graduate from high school.

By the way, I know I'm focusing on math once again, but this action-reaction translates pretty well across other curriculums be they social science, science, English, or PE.

What ends up happening is that site administrators will be pressured by district office administration, who were pressured by the board of education, who were pressured by some parent who showed up to speak at a board meeting to complain that their son or daughter who rarely shows up to class might not graduate; and that something needs to be done about all of the D's and F's that the teachers are giving to their students. And just in case you are wondering, the board will rarely question the parent in regards to the grades and just assume it was the fault of the teachers. This is when site administration will have a meeting with the math department (or any department that is in the same situation) to come up with some sort of plan of action to decrease the number of D's and F's without sacrificing academic rigor. They will then give some long winded, patronizing speech as to how it's not the fault of the department, but that something needs to be done to reduce the number of D's and F's. And even though everyone knows a high percentage of students show up to the high school who barely understand basic fourth and fifth-grade arithmetic (as seen in chapter six), the department is coerced to do something to show they are being "proactive" in dealing with the students that are arriving at the high school unprepared.

By the way, if you aren't in education, whenever RAD says that they don't want to sacrifice academic rigor, they really mean the complete opposite. In other words, dumb down the curriculum as much as you have to in order to decrease the number of D's and F's to keep the ~~customers~~ parents happy.

The department under scrutiny will then have multiple meetings as to what interventions can be used to help these students get to grade level. Please understand that this will not have been the first time that the topic of D's and F's have come up for discussion. This is a normal, annual event where some of the people involved—mostly administrators—seem to have forgotten that a similar conversation was had just twelve months earlier. It has also got to that point where I just don't even bother bringing up that fact that we had attempted (the situation you read about in chapter six was not the first attempt, nor will it be the last) to put something together for struggling students that had no administrative support, which is usually how many solutions to ongoing problems abruptly come to an end; just blowing away with the wind.

"Man up and vanished like a fart in the wind." – Warden Norton (The Shawshank Redemption, 1994)

So instead of having students that have been tested (the results—as you saw earlier—clearly demonstrating that there is a discrepancy when it comes to their understanding of mathematics) showing up to after school tutoring or even attending sessions of Saturday school to catch up, the decision is usually to take the first week or two of the new school year and review as many concepts as possible in order to get all of the students on the same page; sounds good, right? The one obvious flaw in this idea even though administration totally buys it, is that there is no way for students who can barely do 4th and 5th grade arithmetic to catch up on years of mathematics in just one or two weeks.

Let's walk through those first couple of weeks of school for, to say it nicely, a dysfunctional school district. The first two weeks of classes are usually somewhat of a mess. Many classes are way over the limit while some are half empty, and many students are being moved around because they were put into classes that they didn't need just to balance the school's schedule. In other words, lots of students will be moving in and out of classes. This makes some sense as no master schedule is ever perfect from the get-go. The problem is that balancing the classes always takes way longer than it should (three weeks into this year and we're still not done). This is mainly because the district office personnel have to come over and count all the students in the classrooms because district office administration (don't think for a second that they leave their office to come over and count for themselves) do not believe the school's site administration when it comes to the student count. This is usually completed after the first two or three weeks. So yes, about eight percent of the school year is gone before the classes are balanced out.

This shuffling around is usually not too much of an inconvenience when it comes to classroom instruction. Most teachers will start teaching on that first day (yes, I'm that teacher) and others will simply wait by doing word-searches, Sudoku puzzles, or even showing a movie. The reason that they do this is because they will more than likely be getting new students that, if they come in late, will miss the first few weeks of instruction and will already be behind (many students will be coming from a completely different class). Others like me will start on day one, and if someone comes in late then they will have an opportunity afforded to them to catch up on the work that they had missed, but still be held accountable for the work that the other students were already assigned.

So when it comes to the Algebra 1 review that was discussed with the department as a means of helping students catch up to grade level, some teachers won't even get started with it until the second week of class. Ultimately, what ends up happening is that this one or two week review doesn't get done until about the fourth week of school. Not that reviewing is in any way bad for students regardless of the subject, but this always leads to the Algebra 1 classes being behind when it comes to teaching them as well as the nonsensical pacing guides that the district expects the teachers to keep up with.

As the semester progresses, these teachers then realize that they will not be able to get through the material that they were supposed to complete by the end of the first quarter. It is at this point that the teachers will get together and remove certain topics that were supposed to be covered simply because ample time is not available in order to do so. The teachers will then also agree to cut certain topics out of second semester, which will result in even more pot holes when it comes to what is needed for the students to be successful in an Algebra 2 class; if and when they eventually get there.

This clearly leads to an imparity as to what a student should know when they enter an Algebra 2 class, as to what they do know in the same fashion that they entered the Algebra 1 class. What ends up happening here is that the Algebra 2 teacher has to spend the first few weeks of class going over the basics of what these students should have learned in their Algebra 1 class. Then the Pre-Calculus teacher has to spend time reviewing all of the things that the students were supposed to learn in the Algebra 2 class; and so on, and so on, and so on.

As less and less topics are covered in each of the classes (feel free to take this type of situation and apply it to English classes), the end result is that an Algebra 2 class is really not much more than what an Algebra 1 class used to be, and a Pre-Calculus class is no more than what an Algebra 2 class used to be. Now some schools used (most still do but the number of honors classes are also decreasing) to offer honors classes for the small number of students that have shown a desire to advance beyond that of the typical student. But because many of these honors classes are usually smaller when it comes to the number of students, many schools are simply removing them from their schedule of classes.

The reason is very simple as it is, as usual, a matter of money. If a school has five sections of honors classes with twenty or less students, then that is the equivalent of one teacher at a standard six-period day school. By removing those sections and putting the students back into the general classes, that is one less teacher that the district needs to hire and saves the district money. This will be done at the cost of the students who are trying to advance themselves to better prepare for post-secondary education. As usual, if they are able to cut teaching positions, then the district will use that money to hire yet another RAD who will most likely be friends with the superintendent, or maybe the girlfriend of the current board president (no, that's not sarcasm).

———

The question that remains is (which most people already know the answer to): does this tactic of reviewing for the first month or so while foregoing certain topics fix the problems with the number of D's and F's for students in these classes? The answer is *yes*... at least for a couple of years; but not because of the review so much as it is the removing of certain topics (as I discussed) due to lack of time. The number of bad grades will decrease just long enough for everyone to pat themselves on the back and talk about what a great job they are doing because more students are now passing the classes than were before. No one will bring up the fact that the curriculum has been watered down and that grades are higher because students are just repeating, in some instances, what they were supposed to have learned back in the fifth grade, but that's not what's important. The end result is that more students are passing which means they are more likely to graduate and therefore keeping that graduation rate on a steady upslope.

But as I said, this only works for a couple of years. The reason is that after a few years of this, the number of D's and F's will slowly increase using the modified curriculum that was created just a few years back in order to decrease the number of D's and F's. So a new group of students that are failing are doing so with the bar already having been lowered just a couple of years earlier. Thus, the process starts anew once again. The board of education will question the new superintendent (more than likely it won't be the same one as before) who will then question the school site administrators (most, if not all, of whom will be different from just a couple of years ago) who will then have a meeting with whatever department is suffering from an increase in failing students. The end result will be the same as the last time: let's cut out some of the topics of study so that we can spend more time doing less—hence assuring that the students will have a better grasp on what is being taught in the classroom; which is now a watered down version of an already watered down curriculum.

"Insanity: is doing the exact same f#ck!ng thing over and over again expecting sh!t to change. That... is... crazy." – Vaas (Far Cry 3, 2012)

I know I could have just written it the way Einstein *may* have said it originally (I only say it that way as there is some confusion as to whether or not he was the first person to define insanity this way), but you have got to admit that Vaas really knows how to get the point across. Feel free to YouTube "vaas insanity" for the whole speech which, if you are a little older and don't play video games anymore, or perhaps never did, this might be an eye-opener as to how far they have come since the days of the Atari 2600.

So the bar is lowered yet again, grades go up again (even if it just for a few years), the graduation rate remains elevated, and the students enjoy a higher grade-point average—which means their transcripts look better so that they can get accepted to the university of their choice once they graduate from high school. Even though the Pre-Calculus class that they passed is really no more than just an Algebra 2 class at schools that don't cater to educational fads, it still says Pre-Calculus on their transcripts. These students then get accepted to whatever post-secondary school they apply to because all of their college-prep classes have high grades; even though the material that was learned was nowhere near the level of what the class title claims to be.

These students are then accepted thinking that they are ready for the demands of college because they had teachers, counselors, and administrators tell them how amazing they were to get those high grades and how they will do well once they get there. Keep in mind that not all teachers, counselors, and administrators are guilty of doing this, but the ones that tell the truth about the preparedness, or lack thereof, for these students and how it is not going to end well for them are ignored, and are often labeled as negative (yes, that would be me). And if being negative means informing a student who will end up in remedial classes because of a diluted curriculum and keeps them from taking on tens of thousands in student loan debt before the age of twenty, then yes, I am negative.

In the end, what happens to these students once they get to college is that they end up testing into remedial classes and feel that the college is somehow cheating them when, in reality, it was the high school from whence they came that really did them a disservice to begin with. Because of the increase of the number of students that have high GPAs, and transcripts that fulfill the requirements to get into the college, more students are being accepted that are not ready for the demands of the school they were accepted to. They end up doing poorly on the diagnostic exams and are placed into remedial classes, even though they thought they were going to be placed into college level classes instead of those equivalent to that which they took in high school.

The colleges then have to offer more remedial classes resulting in many college professors turning into a high school teacher. See how all of this is connected? Just a small handful of concepts that a student does not understand in elementary school will only compound dramatically as they progress through the educational system. The action that the schools should be taking is to call in the students along with the parents for a meeting and to be honest with them. Tell them the solution is for the student to attend some sort of program to learn that which was not learned originally in order for them to get back to grade level... but they won't. The school will simply catch down to the students instead of having the students catch up to where they should be.

So why not just bring back remedial high school math for students that aren't ready for Algebra 1? Some schools are doing just that. They are reintroducing remedial math into the schedule of classes for the students that struggle with basic arithmetic. And yes, this will be labeled as progressive.

Understand that I am not against having sections of middle school math at a high school (think about that for a moment) in the same fashion that colleges have to offer more and more sections of high school math for the unprepared college students that show up every year. There will always be students that get through who do not understand the basics and should have an opportunity to take a class to help brush up on that which they did not understand the first time. What is perplexing, however, is how the number of section offerings for these lower level classes are increasing year over year at the high school and college levels.

What Nouveau Administration fails to understand, yet again, is that lowering the bar doesn't help the students as they will simply find a way to limbo under it. But that is not their concern. As long as the D's and F's stay off the transcripts and the graduation rate stays at an all time high, then the board of education will also be happy with these results and extend the contract of the current superintendent which will come with yet another raise for a job well done; even though it was really just another act of curriculum manipulation.

Another reason that current administration doesn't care about how the decrease in D's or F's is achieved, or how the graduation rate increases, is because they know they will be gone the next time this lowering of the bar happens again. All that matters is that they will be able to list the data on their résumé so they can brag to the next interviewing committee how they worked yet another cultural-changing miracle.

—

Now there is a situation that some teachers (usually beginning teachers) and observers of the failing educational system might not be aware of when it comes to seniors. This circumstance occurs when a teacher that gives students— specifically seniors for this example—the grades that they earned for a specific class that are either a D or an F. And since a D or F on a transcript might keep a future, unprepared college student from being accepted straight into a four year school, then this might hurt the schools image when it comes to the data that is used as bragging rights for the school and administration.

RAD will deal with this in two different ways. The first will be to coerce the teacher to change the grade. The second—depending on whether or not the teacher will change the grade or stick with it—is to do what is within their power to make certain any teachers who give seniors the D's or F's that they earned, to simply not give them any seniors. This is pretty easy to accomplish as a teacher's schedule is decided by a small group of people consisting of administrators, counselors, and some teachers (usually the sycophantic department chairs). So it is very unlikely that the teacher who gave D's and F's to seniors will no longer be teaching classes that might have seniors enrolled in them. These classes will then be given to teachers who rarely, if ever, fail any students.

RAD simply does not comprehend that when a teacher fails a student who does not show up to class, does not complete assignments, and fails every exam and quiz that they take, is that the F that the student earned—especially when it comes to seniors—is telling them that they are not ready for the next level; especially when that next level comes at a cost of tens of thousands of dollars per year.

- 8 -

Public Perception

It's no secret that every school does all that it can to create and maintain the best possible image for the surrounding community. After all, what parent would want to send their offspring to a school that's tolerant of students ditching class, showing up under the influence of some sort of drug, selling drugs, or teachers that show up late on almost a daily basis? Probably not very many if they knew about the magnitude and frequency in which these things occur. The school I've worked at for nearly two decades is exactly what I just described and then some; I also know that my school is not unique when it comes to these types issues.

So then why would a parent ever send their children to a school like the one I just mentioned? The answer is pretty simple: The majority of parents (even with social media as it is today) simply do not know about the everyday happenings within the confines of the gates of a school. Many schools, especially ones with low parental involvement, are very good at hiding these characteristics. It is these types of schools with low parental turnout at board meetings that also happen to be (more often than not) inner-city, low performing schools.

The public perception of a school is the utmost importance to the local board of education, school site administrators, and especially the overpaid admins over at the district office. The reason is that many parents would be more willing to send their youngsters to a school with a positive image as opposed to a negative one. This forces the school district (mainly the top heavy, six-figure, revolving-door administration) to take measures and do whatever is necessary at each of the school sites within the district to look as good as possible in the eyes of the public that are judging them.

So why are these schools and districts so intent on keeping a positive image? One reason... money. The better a school looks overall to those living in the community the more likely a parent will want to send their son or daughter to that school. And the more students that attend the schools in that district, the more money they [the district but not necessarily the schools] will receive in terms of funding.

Understand that these low-performing school districts will do what is needed to keep a positive image that rarely includes removing certain students from the roll sheets because they are too worried about the loss of funding due to the loss of a student. I'm not talking about the student that has an attitude problem or acts up in class every now and again. I'm referring to those who use and sell drugs during school hours, rarely show up to class, get into confrontations with others students, teachers, administration, and well, anyone else who is on campus at the time.

What administration fails to realize is that as hard as they work to keep one of these students from leaving or, heaven forbid expelling them, the school will lose a number of other students to the school down the road. Most of the time, social media is the means that some parents will find out that said drug selling student will be attending this school and decide to send their children elsewhere, and who can blame them for wanting to do so. The heads of the district are continually scratching their heads and cannot seem to find the reason (although not the only one, but a big one nonetheless) that enrollment has been on a steady decline for a number of years and, for the first time ever since the school opened over fifty years ago, the total number of students attending this school has dropped below one thousand.

At the same school this year, there was one student who was caught multiple times with prescription drugs on his person, as well as other drugs and drug related paraphernalia. Mind you that I'm not talking about one or two pills, I'm talking about bags filled with, in some cases, dozens of these things. Did I mention that this student for at least half of the school year was also an 18 year old adult? So were there any ramifications when he was caught? Absolutely! RAD put his foot down and would give this student, in some cases, a three-day suspension—though most of the time it was only for two days.

But it wasn't just the drugs. This person also had a history of verbally assaulting teachers, administrators (including the principal), support staff, students, and anyone else for that matter. He, at least on two different occasions with two different female employees, left them both in tears after going on a verbal tirade as well as threatening them and yet, the most that would happen to this student would be a few days of suspension, but not always off campus. And even though both women reported the instances to administration, the response was essentially along the lines of a typical, tautological administrative response. And just for emphasis, the student in question was an 18 year old adult.

Lisa: *Judge Snyder, motion to declare a writ of boys-will-be-boys.*

Judge Snyder: *Motion granted. Case dismissed.*

(The Simpsons)

So why did these two women not just call the police? Well, let's just say that this administration has a way of putting people on administrative leave for going over their head with something that could make the school look bad. You'll get a little better idea of this when you get to *Coach's Story*.

For those of you not in education, you might not understand that two days of suspension doesn't mean that the student is off campus for two days. A student could easily be assigned to in-house suspension; which just means that they will sit in an office somewhere on campus under someone's supervision (usually a secretary), and work on assignments that will be sent to the office by the teachers whose classes this student will be missing. The reason for this, once again, is money. As long as the student is on campus, then they are not absent and the school will receive funding for the student for that day.

Another nuance that you might not know about suspensions is that a two day, off-campus suspension doesn't necessarily mean that the student will be off campus for two days. If the suspension occurs early enough, and the parents are notified that same day of the suspension, then that day counts—even though the student will be sitting in an office waiting to be picked up—as the first day of the suspension.

So just pretend that a student threatens a teacher during second period and is pulled out and suspended (let's also pretend that we are at a school that will put teachers' safety in front of ADA) for two days. The parents of the student will be contacted and the student sent home. But because that would count as the first day of the suspension, the second-period teacher that was threatened will only have that student gone from class the next day, and have the student return to class a day later.

I do know for a fact that there are schools out there that would have nipped this in the bud early on and not allow an adult drug user and seller on campus because they are worried about losing funding due to lack of attendance. But because more and more schools are worried about funding, they will do what they can to keep the numbers up; which includes taking and keeping students like the one I just mentioned. They will go out of their way to keep students like these on the attendance rosters, and will only take it to the next level if a parent or parents show up at a board meeting—or someone gets seriously hurt—and make light of the situation; which administration will just pretend they didn't know about and finally take action.

—

Now there are plenty of schools out there that don't have this issue with funding and are under no pressure to take anyone that comes knocking as they not only have great academics, but extracurricular activities as well. These schools not only have fulltime enrollment, but are usually in the business of turning students away, especially if they do not reside within the boundaries of the district—although there's always a workaround to that issue if the student is some sort of superstar athlete.

One common characteristic of schools that have both high academics and athletics is that of parental involvement. These are schools that do well with respect to test scores such as AP, SAT, and whatever state or federal standardized testing is the current focus; or will be in whatever year that you are reading this (this being ~~August of 2017~~ July of 2018 (this one is taking a while)) . As long as a school district has sites within the district with one or both of those characteristics, then they have very little to worry about when it comes to getting students in seats.

Now for schools that do not have great academics or athletics, as well as a problem with drugs or students fighting, then they need to do whatever is necessary to keep the enrollment up to get the students in the seats, and it's this act of filling seats that will keep that flow of money coming out of the educational funding spigot. In other words, these types of schools will take anyone that comes knocking regardless as to why their previous school sent them packing.

Another thing that some parents take into consideration is a school's graduation rate. After all, what parent would want to send their child to a school that has a lower graduation rate than many of the other schools in the area that are the same driving distance away? Then again, they might not be able to send their son or daughter to a different school if it is outside the boundaries of the district. Many people are not aware of this issue, which I will get back to in a little bit.

Now I know I said in the beginning that I would try to avert from talking too much about the disconnect between learning and graduation rates, but being that schools are judged by this rate and the decision for a parent to send their child to a school is at least partially based on this number, I simply can't help myself. The reason is that so many school districts are receiving praise—mainly from themselves—for their graduation rates and very few seem to be asking the means by which these numbers are achieved. So the argument that the graduation rates are not inflated, depending on the perspective of the argument, is valid.

Next time you are on Twitter or Facebook, just search *high school graduation rate* and you will see quite a bit of praise for one school after another on the increase of their graduation rate, but you will also read comments from people who are not so easily fooled by some posted percentage. Some have even achieved that elusive 100% that so many schools are striving towards.

There are plenty of articles out there that claim that the rising graduation rates are not inflated. This I actually agree with from, as I mentioned, a certain perspective. It's important to understand that a school's graduation rate is merely a number based upon how many students at the school complete the necessary units in order to receive their diploma. And this is where the problem lies (you're probably wondering whether or not the pun was intended there).

"And now folks, it's time for: who do you trust?" – The Joker (Batman, 1989)

Take a look at the following graph which compares math and science test scores with that of a school's graduation rate. The question is simple: Which of the schools shown would you trust in regards to their graduation rate being a reflection of learning in contrast to just pushing students through in order to give the perception that learning is taking place?

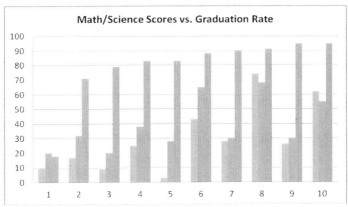

Data courtesy of www.greatschools.org

The bars read from left to right represent the math proficiency scores, science proficiency scores, and the school's graduation rate.

Of the eight schools shown, I would not trust schools seven, nine, and definitely not five. Who would believe a school with less than a five percent proficiency rate for math and nearly a ninety percent graduation rate? Yet, schools like these are praised specifically for that high graduation rate and rarely called out for the means by which that rate is achieved. In other words, it's not really an inflation of the numbers so much as it is a deflation of the academic rigor to achieve said numbers.

The three that I would mostly likely consider to be the more honest schools in the graph shown would be eight, six and one. And when I say honest, I mean schools that do not give in to educational trends such as guaranteeing a minimum of fifty percent for each assignment regardless of attempt.

The problem is that schools such as nine are going to be praised for maintaining a high graduation rate and school one, which is the one I would consider to be most honest if the graduation rate is supposed to be a reflection of learning (I'm starting to question if schools actual consider learning as part of their ontology). More than likely, school one is going to be taken over by the state while school nine is going to celebrate yet again their amazing academic achievements; especially when it comes to the number of students who were accepted to a four-year school. What's not shown is how many of those students end up in remedial classes for their first couple of years all the while accumulating thousands of dollars in student loan debt.

What should really be happening is that not only should the state be looking at what school one is doing wrong and how they intend to improve but, more importantly, why do schools like seven and nine have such a large discrepancy in their proficiency rates with that of their graduation rate? Alas, it is very unlikely that schools like seven and nine will ever be put under a microscope unless their graduation rate suddenly falls or there is some sort of measure of accountability that could disrupt these egregious bifurcations.

In a sense, these questionable graduation rates are very similar to teaching. If a teacher ever has students earning D's and F's that exceed a certain percentage of the number students in the class (that percent totally being whatever RAD wants it to be), then the teacher will be called in for a meeting and have to explain to RAD why there are so many students at the bottom rung of the ladder. On the contrary, if a teacher has nothing but A's, B's, and maybe a few C's, but no D's or F's, then not only will this teacher not be questioned about why the grades are always high (even if test results are abysmal), but this teacher will also be praised at faculty meetings and, more than likely, receive some sort of certificate of appreciation from the principal in regards to what a good job he or she is doing with their students in the classroom.

The problem is that schools like numbers five, seven, and nine, is that they do not really understand what a disservice they are doing to the students that they are graduating (although they are doing a great deal to validate Campbell's law). Many of these students are leaving unprepared for a world that does not care about your grade point average or what your class rank was at your high school. Be it whatever you want to call it, schools like five, seven, and nine are simply committing educational fraud. The administrators that create this situation—whereby a student thinks they are prepared for what comes after graduation simply because they achieved high marks for a watered down curriculum—do not care about the outcomes of their actions (although they will pretend to do so under the guise of one of their favorite phrases: *students first*).

Schools like number nine are simply not being honest with the students that are graduating from their school. But it really doesn't matter to the students who are getting their diploma; or the parents that are cheering in the bleachers on graduation day; and certainly not RAD who will be praised for keeping that graduation rate up near one hundred percent for yet another year. All this does is to help the school to maintain a positive image which will keep up enrollment in order to continue receiving those tax-payer dollars.

"Me I'm dishonest, and a dishonest man you can always trust to be dishonest, honestly. It's the honest ones you want to watch out for. You can never predict if they're going to do something incredibly stupid." – Captain Jack Sparrow (Pirates of the Caribbean: Curse of the Black Pearl, 2003)

Then you have schools like school number one that will be called out for their extremely low graduation rate and yet, I would consider them to be one of the more honest schools whose rate is a real reflection of learning (or not learning depending on your point of view). And even though the truth is right in front of us for all to see, everyone seems content—at least for now— at looking the other way.

The question remains: Why are school like the ones with the obvious divergences as they are, also not called out by the state even though schools like number nine are really not doing much better than school number one? This not only poses a conundrum for schools like number one, but it also gives them a simple solution to keep the feds, the board, parents, and anyone else in the community out of their business. All school number one has to be willing to do is come up with some new *progressive* policy that will allow for the grades of the students to miraculously go higher; all the while the amount of learning stays the same (not that it matters in the eyes of RAD). If they could get their graduation rate up near any of the other schools in that list, then everyone will be happy even though nothing will have really changed with respect to student learning.

It's a sad reality when all a school has to do is change or add a policy (maybe they can borrow the anything less than fifty percent will automatically be changed to fifty percent... or just go straight to sixty) that will yield more A's and B's, but not have to do anything to increase student learning. Suddenly, the graduation rate sky-rockets, and both the school and the local board of education are now praised by the community. Don't be surprised if they also get a nice story in the local newspaper thanks to a simple act of legerdemain.

So will school one fold to the amount of pressure that they are getting from the surrounding community and, more than likely, the state as well? Or will they continue doing what they have been doing which is just telling the truth? Only time will tell; but maybe if other schools were as honest as school one is, then maybe a high school diploma would once again carry with it some value. Yes, they obviously have some major problems, but hopefully they are making an effort to fix the root of the problems instead of paying for some quick fix that one of their administrators will find at a conference.

"People don't want the truth anymore. It's too messy; keeps them up nights." – Harlan Whitford (Safe House, 2012)

So now back to the point that I had brought up earlier about a parent perhaps wanting to send their son or daughter to a school that is in another school district. You would probably think that it would just be as simple as pulling the student out of one district and sending them to a neighboring one. Believe it or not, even though you are the parent, you can actually be turned down for this request.

For starters, many schools are closed to students that do not live within the borders of the district. In other words, if you do not reside within these borders, then your child cannot attend a closed school. And even if the school is open to outside enrollment, they can still turn down the parent as it is their choice to do so as long as the student does not reside in the boundaries of the district.

There is a work-around to this problem of not living within the district boundaries. The solution is to simply use a relative's address that a parent could put onto the enrollment registration form. This "new" address is also needed in order to get the blessing of the current district that the student attends.

For those of you who may not know this, a school district can deny a parent's request to remove their child from their current district in order to have them attend school at another. This rejection from district administration to a parent is quite common; and the reason for declining a parent's request is very simple: money.

As I mentioned earlier, many inner-city, low performing schools are hurting for funding which is a function of (as a colleague once put it) butts in seats. So unless a parent can provide actual proof of living outside of the district, or can afford a good lawyer, the district will simply say *no* to their request. Some districts will go so far as to send someone to validate that the new address is indeed where the family is now living. Feel free to google "school district blocks transfer" and you will get plenty of aggravating stories about district administration turning down a request for a student to transfer out of their district.

Another way around this issue (if using a relative's address or moving is out of the scope of possibilities) would be for a parent to simply send their son or daughter to a private school. But how many parents have the type of income in order to do so?

Suppose that suddenly school district boundaries were removed, and parents were free to send their children to any public school that they choose. The schools that would suffer the most would be those with low graduation rates. Yes, there is a possibility that school nine might lose a few students as some parents are more concerned with academics and might notice the slight discrepancy, but it is because of the low bar, lack of academic rigor, and that high graduation rate that school nine would have students coming from other districts that simply do not want to work hard to earn their high school diploma.

Now take into consideration that with no real form of accountability at the moment, then what is to stop schools like number nine, or five, or any other school in a similar situation, from continuing on their current path, or even lowering the bar some more to keep the enrollment up and the money pouring in from the state? It is with this current lack of accountability that many teachers at these low performing schools will capitulate much earlier than one would expect to. Many teachers that try to keep their standards high for their students will often find themselves having to defend their high expectations in one meeting after another because some student that rarely shows up to class is failing.

RAD simply has it all backwards. Teachers with high expectations that will give a student the grade that they earn (regardless if that grade is an A or an F) should not be the ones who are scrutinized about what they are doing in the classroom. It's the teachers that have an egregious amount of A's and nothing to show for it that should be the ones answering some questions.

So is the graduation rate really that important when it comes to keeping a positive image? Yes, yes it is. It also doesn't hurt that schools like number nine will have just as many graduating seniors being accepted straight to a four-year school than that of their high performing counterpart down the road. At first glance, that is a pretty impressive accomplishment for a school whose proficiency rate in math is a mere twenty-five percent. And every year, schools similar to those of number nine will celebrate all of their students that are graduating even though many of them are doing so are well below grade level.

Mozart: *Herr Zummer? But the man's a fool; he's a total mediocrity!*

Salieri: *No, no, he has yet to achieve mediocrity.*

(Amadeus, 1984)

———

At some point during each school year, every school site will get a few visits from the superintendent; this usually happens at the beginning of each new school year. The subject of the visit normally has to do with the budget and why declining enrollment means that there is just no money available for teachers to receive a raise; even though our administrators have received multiple raises over the last two years. It just seems that when it comes to teachers and other staff members, not only is there never any money, but suddenly we are running some sort of huge deficit that was recently discovered... after administration received their raise, of course.

As a side note, and something I will talk about in the next chapter, the sum of all of those administrative raises could have reduced, or even eliminated, the need for students that attend the school district to have to sell chocolate for at least an entire year.

But now back to the inspirational visit from the superintendent. After being told that there is no money for a raise, RAD will then praise the staff for the wonderful job that they are doing with the students. They will then continue along these lines and mention how school boards and administrators from other districts would call or send emails asking what the school is doing to get so many students to graduate on time. Although no one has said it yet, the answer that RAD should be giving to whomever these people are that are asking about our successes is to respond with the phrase: *academic fraud*.

Obviously, RAD will never admit to that, but at some point a teacher will speak up and definitely use the phrase *academic fraud* (I can assure you that someone is going to be saying it very soon... probably me) when the praise arises for the amazing graduation rate and all of the students that are being accepted straight to a four-year school.

This type of hollow praise happens quite a bit more than you might think. The reason that this praise takes places is to show that administration appreciates the efforts of all of their teachers, and how important of a roll that a teacher plays in the daily life of each of the student. They will then continue talk about how much of a difference each individual plays in the lives of the students that they see every day. The patronizing will continue with more about how all of the accomplishments that have been achieved would not have been possible without the efforts of all the people in the room. I can assure you that there is no sincerity behind the speech.

If you have been in education long enough then you have probably noticed that the more praise district office administration gives to their staff, the worse the news that is about to be delivered. And once the bad news of the district being broke is delivered to the staff and that there is simply no money for support staff or teacher raises (forgetting to mention the fact that administration has already received at least one within the last year), they will then leave the meeting and turn it over to the principal who is in charge of the school and is now left with a room full of staff member who are not exactly in the best of moods.

It is because of your hard work and dedication that we have a 97% graduation rate and so many of our students are going to college.

None of this would be possible without the amazing pedagogical skills that all of you possess.

But I'm sorry to say that because of the two raises administration has received in the last six months, that there is no money for teacher raises.

This act of doing what is necessary to appease the customers (parents and students) within a district will continue as long as school districts do what is necessary to deceive the public when it comes to what is really going on within the walls of the schools. And as long as the majority of people who live within a district choose not to voice their concerns, then this deception of the public will only continue.   Then again, is it really a deception when everyone, for the most part, knows what is going on but are willing to look the other way?

In other words, there are very few people who are unaware (especially in this day and age of instant messaging) of the many schools out there whose graduation rates are increasing, have more students that are being accepted to college because of a watered down curriculum, and also have an increasing number of graduating seniors each year who are well below grade level. Not only that, but there are plenty of these graduates that couldn't handle an eighth-grade curriculum at a middle school that is more concerned about preparing students for the reality of the real world (yes, they do still exist, but RAD will eventually arrive there and shift that paradigm) as opposed to just keeping up the charade of statistics in order to keep the river of money flowing into the hands of the people who need to come up with new methods of perpetuating the ongoing ruse.

Board Agenda
"Students First"

1. Reduce teaching staff by 10% Yes: ☑ No: ☐

2. Reduce the number of counselors from four(4) to two(2) Yes: ☑ No: ☐

3. Hire a new assistant superintendent Yes: ☑ No: ☐

4. Allocate $200k in funding for the new assistant superintendent Yes: ☑ No: ☐

5. Extend the current superintendent's contract by two(2) years Yes: ☑ No: ☐

6. Increase the superintendent's phone and car allowance by 50% Yes: ☑ No: ☐

7. Congratulate ourselves for saving the district money by cutting teachers and counselors Yes: ☑ No: ☐

- 9 -

Selling Chocolate

Fundraising is pretty much a standard practice when it comes to public and private schools; this isn't exactly news to anyone, especially if you're a parent. It is also very likely that you participated yourself way back when, and it's feasible that even as an adult (especially if you are a parent, coach, or both) you are still very active when it comes to helping raise money for a sport, club, or some other activity that is not necessarily school related. Even if you are not a parent or coach, you have probably helped out by buying a lot of whatever it is these kids are selling just to help the cause.

But this act of having to sell something in order to raise money—to say it nicely—irks many people, especially when it comes to our tax-payer funded public school system. If people living within a district, especially parents, ever came to the realization that the amount of money raised through this act of selling chocolate (or anything for that matter) could easily be covered by administrative raises, allowances, or the amount of money that could be saved by removing one of the scheduled conferences that administration will attend throughout the school year, then they might start to attend more board meetings and make a little more noise while attending—especially when it comes to the hiring of another unnecessary revolving door administrator.

Before getting into the aspects of fundraising, I'd like to talk about one issue that is frequently brought up when it comes to funding and education. Often you will find people commenting on social media, board meetings, teacher meetings, or just in everyday conversation that school districts simply need more money in order to be successful. I'm not going to completely disagree as there are some districts that are more than likely underfunded. But the reality is that even if districts were to receive some extra money—for whatever the reason—that it is very unlikely that the extra dollars would make it to where it is supposed to be going: the students.

"We can put that check in a money-market mutual fund. Then we'll reinvest the earnings into foreign currency accounts with compounding interest... and it's gone." – Bank Clerk (South Park)

In other words, the majority of any extra money, if not all, will disappear as it slowly funnels through the chain of bureaucracy over at the district office.

Now for private schools it makes a little more sense to have to raise money as they [the private schools] are dependent on the parents that pay the tuition for their children. Some schools, especially the ones with well known athletic programs, have very little problem when it comes to getting however much money is necessary to run a school for the year, or build a new gym for their nationally-renowned basketball program. So in the sense of a privately funded school that is dependent on parents and private contributions, then raising money by selling something or through some charity event makes more sense than it does for their public school counterparts.

But what doesn't make sense is that students from a public school, funded by tax-payer dollars, often have to appeal for funds from the surrounding communities in order to raise money for that which is needed in regards to the activity that they represent. Possibly more irksome is the frequency by which the students have to take part in these fundraising activities.

Granted, it is not exactly feasible to pay for all of the extra things that clubs and sports might need; especially when it comes to something that might not be an immediate necessity. There isn't some magical crystal ball that helps to foresee the extra expenses that may unexpectedly come along during a school year. There are, however, certain facets of these extracurricular activities such that no student should have to spend their time selling candy in order to raise money for— such as soccer balls for the soccer team. There is a very high likelihood that the funds are already available, but have simply been misallocated towards another administrative position, an increase in the superintendent's car or cell phone allowances, or some new educational piece of software that someone at the district decided to purchase for all teachers to use regardless of need.

Now there are some administrators, believe it or not, that have actually turned down a raise. Yes, they are out there—the population is very few and far between—but they do exist. And just in case you don't believe me, the next time you visit your favorite search engine, just search for "school administrator turns down raise". You will get some hits (although not as many if you search for "school board mismanages funds"), honestly!

If you are that person by the way, then kudos to you for doing what so many never even consider doing when it comes to increasing their pay.

—

Whether or not you want to admit it, there are some clubs or sports that do receive more funding (not always proportionally) when it comes to the needs of a specific club or sport simply because of their popularity. This, then again, isn't exactly anything new to anyone, anywhere.

"Before I sing the national anthem, I'd like to say that college football diverts funds badly needed for education and the arts." – Lisa Simpson (The Simpsons)

The question that people should be asking is this: Why, for many of the activities regardless of whether it's the football team or the chess club (I would add books or science lab equipment to that list, but I have yet to learn of an instance where a student had to sell chocolate in order to purchase books and other classroom necessities, at least for a public school, but it would also not surprise me if it has happened), is there so little funding when it comes to many of the extra-curricular activities? Then follow that up with: *How is it the local board of education always seems to find money needed for a conference or a new administrative position?*

With top-heavy administration running the districts, and the board of education always able to find and allocate money to hire yet another six-figure administrator, you might think that finding a few hundred dollars to help out any of the activities, be they popular or not, would be just as easy. Alas, as you know, it is not. Well it is, but it just seems very difficult for the board to do so when it comes to something they don't consider to be necessary because selling chocolate will take care of it.

And this is where the fundraising aspect comes into play. You have all seen it, and many of you will help out (thank you, by the way) by buying more than your share of goodies from a student in order to make their lives easier when it comes to obtaining the necessary funding for whatever the activity is that they are part of.

Every year, students walk around with boxes of chocolate, or order forms usually containing some sort of sugar laden edible for you to purchase just in time for the holiday season. More than likely (especially if you have kids of your own) you are very familiar with this process. If you are a parent, then you have probably brought boxes of chocolate, or these order forms, to your place of employment and hit-up the people that hit you up earlier in the year as a matter of quid pro quo.

But why (in public a school) is this even necessary on the scale that it is as well as so commonplace? I can understand that occasionally extra funds are needed for an event that was not on the initial itinerary of the club or sport and some extra money needs to be raised. We all understand that happens, but I'm not talking about these one-off instances.

Year after year, I will see the same students carrying around boxes of chocolate for the clubs or sports in which they participate. Aside from athletics, it's not like the Academic Decathlon team, the Math-Engineering-Science-Achievement (MESA) club, or the chess club, are anything new to many districts. And yet, as much as administration pushes for these activities, there just never seems to be enough money to help fund them, but there's just about always enough money to hire yet another six-figure administrator to inform the district of some problem that we already know of; such as the existence of an achievement gap.

"No $hit, Sherlock." – Audrey II (Little Shop Of Horrors, 1986)

This brings up the question: Why the district is not able to allocate funds for the main expenses for each of the extracurricular activities that a school has to offer its students? More often than not, the person in charge (most of the time a teacher) is reduced to begging for money that is necessary for whatever the activity is that they are in charge of. They will go to different organizations such as ASB (Associated Student Body), SSC (School Site Council), or even local shop owners for money to help fund necessities be they band uniforms or soccer balls.

So are school districts really that broke to the point that they can't come up with a few hundred dollars to help out students that the received monies are supposed to be supporting to begin with? Well, if you believe those at the top, then *yes* is the answer. But we all know that (unless the district is in dire financial status which, if you believe the board and the top brass, they always are) the money is there, it's often just being spent in all the wrong places. And if a district's financial state is really to the point of insolvency, then there is a pretty good chance that the feds have already been snooping around the district office.

Take into consideration that many of these fundraisers, for the most part, might be lucky enough to bring in maybe one or two hundred dollars being that the profit margin on a candy-bar is razor thin. So a club with ten students (just as an example) may bring in one or two hundred dollars for an entire fundraiser which might cover the cost of transportation to a couple of events or maybe some updated uniforms. Multiply this by four of these per year, and a club (depending on the size of the school, the club, and a slew of other factors, but you get the point) might be able to bring in four to eight hundred dollars for the entire year (eight being very unlikely for a club with only ten students).

So why is it so easy for a local board of education to find money to pay for another person to add to the already overloaded set of administration, or send administration to yet another 3-day, 2-night, all expenses paid conference where rooms can easily run $300+ per night? And yet they can't find money to help out a team or club (or a department in need of new books as the ones they currently use are well over a decade old) when they are in need of some extra funds for equipment or uniforms.

Now let's do a little more arithmetic. Let's take one six-figure administrator off of the payroll. This could be a district office administrator or a vice principal at one of the school sites. For the sake of this example, let's take a look at one of the most useless (and that is saying a lot for my district) vice principals that our district has ever hired. Also understand that I have worked with at least twenty different vice principals in eighteen years with this district; so to say this person was useless is not hyperbole. Through just a little research, and thanks to the website www.transparentcalifornia.com, I was able to find that this person's salary plus benefits came to a little more than $135,000. Just for emphasis, if this person never showed up to work, no one would ever notice.

Just imagine what that $135k could do for all of the extra-curricular activities as well as the classrooms on campus. Now, there are those that might like to make the argument that this wouldn't be possible because certain monies are earmarked for certain areas of spending. This is true; but if you are in education, or any field for that matter, then you also know that the board and whoever the lackey of the board is, will find a way to move that money around to wherever they see fit. There are always loopholes somewhere in the wording that allows for those in charge to find some sort of work-around to shuffle the money to wherever it is they want it to go.

—

Very often, especially on social media, there are comments from people in regards to increasing the funding that school districts receive from the state. There will also be lots of support for these comments as to how more money will benefit those that the money is supposed to be helping to begin with. I have yet to be witness to a comment from a non-political individual that is in support of cutting educational funding; though there are plenty regarding the spending of said funds.

What is important to understand is that more often than not, the funding is actually there. It just manages to be dispersed and disappear through different avenues before it gets to where it is supposed to be going. Or perhaps it is allocated towards an "expensive tool" in the form of some piece of software that someone over at the district office decided all of the teachers need to start using without first talking to the teachers to see if it would be benefit the students.

"In education we subsidize the producer, we subsidize the school. If you subsidize the student instead, you would have competition. The student could choose which school they would go to, and that would force the schools to improve and to meet the tastes of their students." – Milton Friedman

School district spending works, or doesn't depending on one's perspective, in a similar manner as trickle-down economics. Give the taxpayer dollars to a small cohort of people running the district and let them decide how to allocate said monies—under the premise of *students first*—but after they take what they consider to be their fair share. Then again, this is really nothing new to anyone. The whole idea of educational spending has been a point of controversy for as long as education has been around.

If you do a little math, you will find that in some districts the pay of the top four or five administrators alone could eat up almost five percent of the district's annual budget, or possibly even more. For example, the top four at my current district of employment cost the district over a million dollars per year when you include salary, medical benefits, and allowances such car, cell phone, cost of sending them to multiple multi-day conferences during an academic year, and any other details that were snuck into their contract.

One possible solution that has been a heated topic of debate for many years is that of the school voucher. I'm not saying that vouchers (or some variation of) are *the* solution to the problems when it comes to educational funding, but it is something that is definitely worth discussing. A little research will show that the idea of a school voucher goes back easily a couple of centuries.

I am also familiar with the school voucher controversy that goes back to the '60s regarding the Brown v. Board of Education outcome, which often leads people to oversimplify the origins of the voucher system being deeply rooted in racial segregation, and it can easily be argued that they are, but that's like saying that water fountains are inherently a bad idea because they were once used to racially segregate society. I am simply using it as an example to show that the top-down model is not working as it stands and though vouchers sound nice on the surface, we'll probably end up right back where we started.

It is also important to understand that the court decision of Brown v. Board of Education did not result in the idea of the school voucher. The idea of subsidizing the student instead of the producer when it comes to education has roots going back a few centuries. Here is a little excerpt from Thomas Paine's collection *The Rights of Man* back in 1791: "*To pay as a remission of taxes to every poor family, out of the surplus taxes, and in room of poor-rates, four pounds a year for every child under fourteen years of age; enjoining the parents of such children to send them to school, to learn reading, writing, and common arithmetic."*

If that isn't enough for you, then fast forward sixty-eight years to John Stuart Mill's essay *On Liberty;* still ninety-five years before the Brown v. Board of Education decision: *"If the government would make up its mind to require for every child a good education, it might save itself the trouble of providing one. It might leave to parents to obtain the education where and how they pleased, and content itself with helping to pay the school fees of the poorer classes of children, and defraying the entire school expenses of those who have no one else to pay for them."*

Now one can easily argue that those were just thoughts by a couple of men that penned the idea, but never put them into practice. I understand this, but was just using them as an example to demonstrate that the idea has been around longer than many people think. In fact, if you really want to delve a little deeper, the first instance of school vouchers being put into practice came in 1944 to help those returning from serving their country in World War II—you know this as the G.I. Bill. This bill provided a voucher to veterans upon return who were interested in attending college and allowed them to enroll in the college of their choice.

The underlying idea of the voucher does sound very nice; give the money in the form of vouchers to the students as opposed to the districts. And as there have been plenty of books and papers written on school choice, I really do not want to write an entire dissertation on what plenty of people have already done. Nor am I saying that vouchers represent the absolute solution to the educational epidemic (although one could easily argue pandemic).

Being that I have only been part of the trickle-down educational system both as a student and as a teacher, I can say that trying something else might lead to a change for the better (I bet you thought I was going to say *paradigm shift*) as opposed to the system as it currently stands, which only seems to be getting worse.

But here's a thought: Could the voucher system actually do away with the majority of fundraising that students have to partake in year after year? Well, that would depend on what type of system we are talking about. If all we do is switch over to the voucher system but leave the same people in charge, then there really is no need for the change as those at the top will be the same people deciding how to spend the money that is brought into the district.

So are the vouchers the answer to some of the problems that ail our system as it stands? Without a decent sample size it's hard to say. Plenty of people thought that the solution was going to be the charter school system, but being that there is enough evidence that they [charters] haven't proven to be any more effective than the system that is currently in place, then maybe it is time to try something else.

Now put the idea of vouchers together with that of a headless school (you might want to google that one), and suddenly there would be competition for not only students to attend a specific school, but districts would now have to compete to bring in the best teachers so that parents and students will want to attend a school in their district. Since site administration duties are divided amongst the teachers for a headless school, then suddenly those overpaid administrators who sit back in their chair and delegate their responsibilities to someone else will also be out of a job, and deservedly so.

Once again, vouchers sound good on the surface, but even if they are one possible future path, there will be (as there always is) problems from day one. Will they be perfect? No. Will there be fraud (just google "school voucher fraud")? Of course there will be; we are talking about the public education system here. Will it be worse than it is now? That's very difficult to say without doing a very detailed analysis of those districts that utilize that type of system. And yes, if you've been doing this long enough, it can definitely be worse.

By the way, if you do work in education then you have probably had that discussion with colleagues as to whether or not it could be worse when a new administration moves in. And as it has probably happened to you as it has to me, just when you think the next administration can't possibly be as inept as their predecessors, they will find a way to prove us wrong... again.

As a side note, the fact that wasteful spending and fraud are just accepted to be part of the educational construct— regardless as to whether you are talking about a traditional, charter, or voucher system (a little googling will yield plenty of results irrespective of the type of system)—demonstrates that maybe we're all looking in the wrong place to help fix the problems of the system, and that maybe we should start by curbing, and possibly eliminating (I'll be the first to admit that completely eliminating fraud is nearly impossible), the amount of mismanaged monies that now seems to be the norm when it comes to the education system.

—

Vouchers represent just one of the many options that are currently available. But there is also a very high likelihood that the local school board and superintendent (along with his or her lackeys) will do just what they've been doing and spend the money how they want to spend it regardless; leading to a similar version of the system as it is at the moment. In other words, the fraud and manipulation will still be rampant because the same people in control of the money for our current system will be the same people in control of the money for the voucher system.

"Lesson number one: don't underestimate the other guy's greed."
– Frank Lopez (Scarface, 1983)

As it stands, the people in charge of the money are the ones at the top. I know this from personal experience as administrators at our school district have received multiple raises over the last couple of years (some of these admin have only been in the district for a couple of years) all the while adamant that there isn't enough money available to hire more teachers. At what point does the board of education and administration start telling teachers to sell chocolate to help raise money to pay their own salaries? Although I say that in jest, how far are we from something like that actually happening?

After all is said and done, it seems as if there are options to cut-down, or get rid of entirely, this need for students to go out year after year to sell something that could easily be covered by the cost of one administrator. Many of these school districts could easily afford to cut one of the many useless administrative positions. That savings of $135k that I mentioned earlier of a person who got the job because of his relationship with the superintendent, would add up to over $1M in just over seven years. And just to stress this once more, if this person never showed up to work, no one would have noticed.

The one year of savings (you could also imagine if that same money was kept specifically in a fund and allowed to accrue interest year over year as long as no administrator is hired for that money) could easily fill the gaps for any unforeseen expenses that clubs, sports, or class (buying breakfast for AP students that come in on a Saturday for a practice test or study session, for example) that may be incurred during a school year. It is also very likely that there would be leftover money that could carryover for multiple years. I can honestly say that for the price of one administrator (someone really needs to infomercial this) no student in many of the surrounding districts would have to sell any chocolate, or participate in any fundraising for that matter, for easily two or three years. And that is just with one year of saving $135k wasted on that particular administrator who left the district for a higher paying job as the current pay and benefits was just not enough for him. He was also the same administrator that you will read about in *Coach's Story*.

So if you didn't really think much of this particular person, and those of the same ilk (as he is just one example of many that exists within the school system), then just wait; you will dislike him much more after you read Coach's Story.

The question that people (especially parents) should be asking themselves is: *Can a school district function just as well if they had one less administrator at a school site or the district office?* I can assure you that the answer is a resounding *yes*. The problem is that many parents, especially those who reside in an inner-city, lower performing school district, rarely question the decisions of the local board of education and the superintendent in regards to hiring practices, mostly because they simply don't know about those practices. It is just assumed that those running the district who are making these decisions are weighing all of the opportunity costs of the money that needs to be allocated to pay for a six-figure position, or to attend that three day conference where admin dine on $48 dollar rib eye steaks (you have to assume they don't enjoy fork-tender meat because they're always in favor of making cuts...).

And even if for some reason one or two administrative positions were to be cut to save the district money (as for some reason districts always seem to be in dire-straights), not one person sitting on the board, or the superintendent, or one of the people brought in by the superintendent, will suggest that the money be put into a fund to be used in lieu of selling chocolate.

———

So let's pretend for just a moment there is a competent school board at some district in some state that do not hire their friends and put people they know into high paying administrative positions after a sham of an interview process. Now let's suppose that the board comes to the realization that they really do not need all of the administrators that they have on contract, and also understand that the money saved by letting one go could be used to curb, or even eliminate fundraising while concurrently allowing some teachers to earn a little extra money.

Suppose that you were to eliminate the vice principal in charge of curriculum. The first question that might be asked from someone who has not been part of the educational system is: *who would do all of the work that this person does*? By the way, if you work with RAD, then I don't blame you if you just laughed out loud.

If you have been part of the system as long as I have, then it's very probable that you have had the pleasure of working with more vice principals (regardless of what the title of their position is) than you can count. Personally, I have worked with four different vice principals in charge of curriculum over the last six years. And yes, there are certain facets of their job that are an absolute must such as taking care of the logistics for AP testing (which, if it wasn't for the AP teachers and their experience, would be an absolute mess this year) or creating the school's master schedule of classes. But I can assure you that a person does not need an administrative credential to handle these aspects of a school. It's usually counselors who do master scheduling, and test coordination is often covered by, well, sometimes it's hard to figure out who exactly is in charge of all of the testing; but what I can tell you is that, at least at my school, the secretary of the curriculum office pretty much ran the gamut this year, and did one hell of a job doing so.

It's highly probable that many curriculum administrators have not been out of the classroom for very long, and their knowledge of handling these types of issues will not be any more substantive than someone that is still in the classroom. So if this particular person is no longer on the payroll, then who will perform the tasks that are usually handled by this administrator? Well, here's a thought: let some of the teachers do it.

Let's do a little arithmetic. According to transparent California (www.transparentcalifornia.com), this specific admin position—salary plus benefits—cost the district about $135k annually (same as the discipline administrator as I mentioned earlier). The district could easily take a fraction of that money and create some very generous stipends for a small committee of teachers that would be willing to take on an extra assignment, such as organizing AP or CC testing. In other words, in a similar fashion to a teacher taking on an extra teaching assignment when another section of a class opens up but does not warrant the need to create another teaching position, then whoever the teacher is that is willing to take on the extra class is able to earn some additional money in lieu of having a conference period. Yes, it is more work, but there would be plenty of teachers (or the secretary that will stay late and show up early to do the work that an administrator is being paid to do) willing to take on some extra work if they are fairly compensated for their time.

The same strategy could be used to divide the responsibilities of that one administrator that every campus has who, if they never showed up to work, no one would even notice was missing. A district could easily take $30k of that $135k and divide it amongst 6 teachers who are willing to take on the obligations of that person that occur throughout the year. This would not only give some teachers on campus an opportunity to earn some extra money, but also spread out the responsibilities for these teachers such that the tasks are not too overwhelming for them to complete for the school year. And if for some reason they screw up their part, then they do not receive most, if not all, of the stipend and can no longer apply for that specific position.

Please understand that I am not saying that an administrator is the equivalent of six teachers (as they still have their classes to teach). I am merely suggesting that the responsibilities could be divided up in such a way as to not be overly cumbersome for the teachers who take on the extra work to where it impedes on their daily classroom activities.

So what to do with the other $105k? Not only would that leftover amount eliminate the need to fundraise for all schools in my district (I can't speak for others, but I'm pretty sure that this amount of money would have a similar impact) with quite a bit left over, but maybe, just maybe, the history department could finally get some up-to-date books. And even with the purchasing of new books, and fundraising eliminated so that students will no longer have to carry around boxes of chocolate or some other types of confections, there will more than likely still be some leftover money that could easily be used for other necessities that many schools are lacking, or even hiring another teacher.

Though there is some *raison d'être* for fundraising (as I mentioned a few pages back) when it comes to unexpected expenses, the majority of it (if not all) could easily be removed from the itinerary of a student who wants to participate in something that goes beyond that of a typical school day—if the local board of education would take a little more time and effort in deciding how the annual funding is allocated. But I wouldn't be holding my breath for any nascent, meaningful changes to occur anytime soon.

- 10 -

Standards Based Learning

One of the first things I found strange as a new teacher back in the early 2000s, was being told that there were specific items that needed to be taught throughout the year. I was given a pacing guide with a bunch of items that needed to be covered in the classes I was teaching. This was a little bit of an eye opener for me as I wondered who the people were that went through an algebra book and chose certain topics that they felt were important and omitted others that they felt were not. These items, or standards as I quickly learned that they were called, were somewhat of a head-scratcher when it came to teaching (we were using the Integrated Math at the time; which was even more of a head-scratcher to me) a pre-algebra, algebra, or any math class for that matter.

For my first year of teaching, I clearly had the class schedule that no one else wanted (which is pretty much the norm and a rite of passage—with very few exceptions—for a new teacher). I had five sections of remedial math of at least twenty-five students, but no more than thirty-six; nearly all of which struggled with basic number sense. And when I say struggled with number sense, I'm talking about 9th and 10th graders who couldn't tell you that fifty percent of forty is twenty. But keep in mind that many schools have graduating seniors who could also not tell you that fifty percent of forty is twenty (see my previous book).

The idea of teaching certain topics in a math class that someone else deemed important over other topics seemed a little strange. There were obviously some pretty dramatic changes in teaching during that five or six years that I had transitioned from a high school student to that of a high school teacher.

So what happened after I graduated high school that suddenly turned teaching an entire subject, to just focusing on a specific number of topics in said subject? As it turns out, the topics that were targeted to be taught in the classroom were decided by different administrators mainly, at the time, located at the district office.

All of this actually goes back to my senior year in high school. Although it had no bearing on anyone in my graduating class or the next couple of classes, I do recall that there was a lot of fuss over the freshmen at the time. The fuss being over the new state testing that was going to start with that particular freshman class. What happened was that the state of California (along with pretty much every other state) decided to create some end of the year testing to try and figure out what was happening in the classrooms of schools around the state. Up until this started, it was up to each site to set their own measures of accountability... kind of.

These End-of-Course (EOC) exams would be taken by all students with the exception of seniors. The exams taken by the students would be in the core classes of math, science, English and social science. The students would then take whatever test matched the class that they were taking at the time. But this testing of students in at least math and English was not really anything new. In fact, many schools had their own exams that students had to pass in order to graduate before standardized testing, as we currently know it, came along.

If you went to school anytime before the year 2002, at least in the state of California, then it is very likely that you took proficiency exams (these exams did overlap for a few years with the standardized testing that was being implemented) in math and English that were created by the school that you attended. The official title for these was the High School Competency Exams. Aside from clearly being created before acronyms became all the rage, these exams were the result of California law passed back in 1978. Each school created their own set of exams that had to abide by the rules of content and reporting as put forth by the state. The reason that schools, at least in California, discontinued these exams is because of the implementation of the STAR (Standardized Testing and Reporting) program and eventually the now defunct California High School Exit Exam (CAHSEE).

And if you did go to school before the year 2000, then it was very unlikely that you had certain standards posted on the board to indicate what you had to know for some specific standardized test. Yes, most teachers had something written down when it came to what was going on for the day (referred to as a Content Objective in today's educational world), but these topics weren't impelled on both the students and teachers as something that if not covered would somehow be detrimental to life itself.

"Let's go over the rundown for the week." – Dave Medrano (Spanish and Humanities teacher)

It was also around this time that many of those classes that students would take as electives (drafting, accounting, and woodshop, just to name a few) in the hopes of learning a marketable skill before graduation, started to disappear from a school's schedule of course offerings. Schools needed to start making room for more core classes that focused on these EOC exams. So many of the electives that served no explicit purpose when it came to improving test scores simply had to go.

Now, since the state did not want to leave the schools in the dark regarding what the students were going to be tested on, they released a blueprint of topics that were going to be covered for each subject and test. And thus, standards based teaching was born.

As per anything in education, there were plenty of proponents and opponents to standards based teaching and testing. It is important to understand that the tests that these students were taking at the end of the year did not have to change how the subjects were being taught. The problem was that many schools decided that the only things that were suddenly worth teaching, were those mentioned in the standards put forth by the state.

So what ended up happening is that schools and districts got their hands on these standards and started using them to create a base for the entire curriculum for each of the core subject areas. This was the point that RAD decided that the only things that should be taught were those that were dictated by the state.

Bill Moyers: *You think there are too many tests? We give kids too many tests?*

Neil deGrasse Tyson: *I think we put too much emphasis on what the meaning of the test is.*

(Bill Moyers interview with Neil deGrasse Tyson)

Ultimately, these set of standards suddenly went from being just some guidelines for the End-of-Course testing at the end of the year, to the whole basis for teaching each subject. This was also the point where the whole *teaching to the test* problem really started to gain momentum.

Now there were plenty of people that saw this coming. After all, if you can remember that far back, the state was giving very nice financial awards to teachers when the students as a whole for a specific school did well on the exams. To anyone with some good sense, this act of giving egregious bonuses (I heard as high as $10k per teacher at schools that scored very well) to all the teachers at a specific school—if the students as a whole exceeded the degree of expectations when it came to their scores—would obviously lead to only more teaching to the test.

This act of giving bonuses only lasted a few years (the last of the bonuses being given out after the fourth or fifth year, which turned out to be my first year in the classroom) for the obvious reasons. The first being that the state would be broke very quickly if they continued to give that much money away. The second, well, did they really think if these bonuses were tied to test scores that there wouldn't be some form of cheating involved? There are plenty of stories on the internet regarding cheating on standardized tests which shouldn't really be too surprising with the amount of emphasis that is put on the results (feel free to look up Campbell's law). One principal in my district was actually fired for knowingly allowing some cheating to occur. Remember, administrators don't have tenure, so the act of releasing them is a much easier process than that of a teacher.

———

This act of just teaching a targeted number of specific topics (in the business it's called "targeting the standard") also made it easier with respect to creating a preset path on what needed to be covered for teachers, administrators, and the students. Think about, isn't it a lot easier for an algebra teacher to model a problem that they know is going to be on the test, then give a bunch of similar problems to the students so that they can regurgitate the same steps to get the right answer? It doesn't really help the students to understand why that specific algorithm works for that type of problem, or help them to figure out and understand that there might be different possibilities to solve the problem; but hey, it gets the right answer every time.

There is that obvious question that goes along with this whole idea of teaching to the test, which is: *Is it really teaching or learning if all one is doing is conditioning a student to memorize something that has a high probability of appearing on the test at the end of the year?* Is the approach of: *here is a problem and this is how you do it,* when they [the students] take the test at the end of the year the best approach to the educational process? I'd like to think the answer is *no*, but with more and more schools jumping onto the *standards-based instruction to get a good score for the test at the end of the year* bandwagon, then I could easily be wrong about this educational technique. But just because there is a possibility that I am wrong, doesn't mean that I'm going to suddenly give in to a long standing education faux pas.

The only teachers that have problems when it comes to the teaching to the test mantra are those like me that don't believe that this approach to education is in any way beneficial to the students in the long run. It doesn't create problem solvers, critical thinkers, or people that can come up with their own algorithms to solve a problem instead of just being given one that works. In the end, this approach to teaching ends up creating generations of students that can tell you that 2x3 = 6, but couldn't tell you why with respect to the definition of multiplication as it pertains to addition.

So back to why going against this teaching to the test makes the life of some teachers even more difficult than it already is. It's not really that not doing it is the problem; it's speaking up against it that can cause some issues. So if you are a Neophyte (which you'll read about in the next chapter) and you don't want to teach to the test, then don't; but your life will be much easier if you just don't verbally oppose teaching only specific standards in your classroom.

Now you might be thinking, won't RAD know if I am or am not teaching a specific math, or any subject for that matter, standard (veteran teachers just had a really good laugh)? Of course they won't. The only time this might happen is if you have a former math or science teacher as an administrator; which, if they do have that background, then there is a high probability that he or she will agree with the damage caused by only teaching to the test.

For example, if you teach Algebra 1 and you are able to cover the majority of sections (it is very rare that any teacher or professor anywhere covers every single section of a book) in the book that you are using, then it is very likely that you also covered all of the standards that needed to be addressed for the year. I would go so far as to say that a school with good teachers, regardless of the subject matter, that focus on problem solving and allowing the students to figure out solutions based on their own logic—instead of just repeating algorithmic steps—wouldn't even need to look at the Common Core standards in order for their students will do well.

"The code is more what you'd call guidelines than actual rules." – Barbossa (Pirates of the Caribbean: The Curse of the Black Pearl, 2003)

The point is that the standards put forth by the state, or whoever is in charge of doing so, are not the problem. The problem is that those hired to micromanage curriculum for a school district are the ones who are creating this teaching to the test mentality; which only gets worse as the years progress. These are the people who simply do not understand the connection between something that is learned in a fourth-grade math class, and how it can be tied to something that is taught in an Algebra 2 class.

One main reason that RAD is making it worse is that they will walk through classes and check to see if what is being taught is based on the standards. Some admin will actually take a list of standards to classrooms in order to verify that teachers are indeed covering what is on the list that someone over at the district office created. Some of these pacing plans do break things down by week; so if you are being evaluated by one of these micromanaging administrators, then you better be where the pacing guides tell you that you need to be, or you will likely receive a negative evaluation or, at the very least, some negative comments on your walkthrough results.

Pro tip for Neohpytes, or even seasoned veterans, if you don't want to teach to the test, but you want to keep RAD off your case (no one will blame you for that) in regards to not teaching directly to the standards that some person gave to you, then just put a content and language objective on your board and leave it there. The majority of them are so clueless that you could put an economics standard on the board for your math classes and they will check it off every single time they do a walkthrough. You might want to consider changing it every now and then, but it's very unlikely that any of them would even notice.

Even more important to understand is that whatever the

standards are at any given time, it's very likely they will be more convoluted than the previous set of standards and are even more useless to a teacher. Just as an example, if I had only taught specifically to the standards when we did have our state testing, then I would have taught logarithmic functions without first teaching exponential functions. And just in case you might not be up to date on your Algebra 2 topics, doing so would be equivalent to teaching division without first teaching multiplication, or subtraction without first covering addition.

Chapter 6 Exponential Functions and Sequences	A.CED.2 Graph equations on coordinate axes with labels and scales.
6.1 Exponential Functions. (A.CED.2, F.IF.4, F.IF.7e, F.IF.9, F.BF.1a, F.BF.3, F.LE.1a, F.LE.2)	F.IF.4 For a function that models a relationship between two quantities, interpret key features of graphs and tables in terms of the quantities.
6.2 Exponential Growth and Decay. (A.CED.2, F.IF.7e, F.IF.9, F.BF.1a, F.BF.1b, F.LE.1c, F.LE.2)	F.IF.7e Graph exponential and logarithmic functions, showing intercepts and behavior.
6.3 Compare Lin. & Exp. Functions. (F.IF.6, F.BF.1a, F.LE.3)	F.IF.9 Compare properties of two functions.
6.4 Solving Exponential Equations. (A.CED.1, A.REI.1, A.REI.11)	F.If.6 Calculate and Interpret the average rate of change of a function over a specified interval. Estimate the rate of change from a graph.
Project introduction.	F.LE.2 Construct linear and exponential functions, including arithmetic and geometric sequences, given a graph, a description of a relationship, or two input-output pairs.
6.5 Geometric Sequences. (F.IF.3, F.BF.1a, F.BF.2, F.LE.2)	
6.6 Recursively Defined Sequences. (F.IF.3, F.BF.1a, F.BF.2, F.LE.2)	
Chapter 7 Data Analysis and Display	F.BF.2 Write arithmetic and geometric sequences both recursively and with an explicit formula.
7.4 Two-Way Tables. (S.ID.5)	S.ID.5 Summarize categorical data

Now let me show you how ridiculous it is getting with respect to the micromanagement of what some person over at the district office decides what topics are important to teach. The previous picture is based on standards that they find on some website somewhere, and put them down into a pacing guide as to what the math teachers at a school are supposed to be teaching. The picture represents about forty percent of the third quarter of Integrated Math 1 (think first year algebra with a little mix of geometry and basic statistics). Keep in the back of your mind the results of the diagnostic exam that was in chapter

6, as well as the grade level of questions that were on the exam.

Sorry about the small font. It was much smaller on the initial document, but it looks like gibberish regardless of the size of the font that is used. Words honestly can't describe how asinine it is for anyone to expect students who have trouble with fourth and fifth-grade arithmetic to be able to learn, understand, and are expected to retain from a pacing plan that was put together by a person who has never taught a day of mathematics in their life.

For starters, don't feel bad if you don't know what a lot of the abbreviations mean. I teach math, have a degree in it, and I don't know what they mean, nor do I care what they mean.

As ridiculous as that list might seem, do not blame Common Core for it. The fault lies with those administrators over at the district office that put people in charge of deciding what is, or is not important for a student to learn, and the time frame for them to learn it in. The person or persons who created this are handpicking standards that they think are important based on the Common Core standards, but do not fully—or at all in most cases—understand how time is needed to really comprehend more than the surface value of a topic for the sake of being able to recognize it on a test.

Regardless if you are a math teacher or not, you probably understand how difficult it would be to get through the topics from the list in a three to four-week period of time if this were an Algebra 2 class. Also notice the sudden change from student recursive defined sequences to two-way tables as it pertains to data analysis.

As I mentioned, it would be tough enough for the teacher and students to get through those topics in an Algebra 2 class, nonetheless an Integrated Math 1 class which, as you saw in chapter 6, many of the students had trouble with fourth and fifth-grade arithmetic. RAD's perception that these topics can be taught to students who have not only struggled for years, but have also been taught math through memorization of algorithms to get answers is delusional to say the least.

"This is so nuts. I mean listen... listen to what you're saying; it's paranoid delusion. It's really sad; it's pathetic." – Carter Burke (Aliens, 1986)

I'm really starting the think that Ripley (from Alien and Aliens) was really a teacher and the xenomorphs were administrators. The whole thing took place during some sort of professional development training on how to turn a computer on and off; and the fifty-seven years was actually a fifty-seven minute nap that was interrupted by RAD tapping her on the shoulder and asking her to demonstrate that she knew how to turn on and off the computer that was assigned to her.

—

This method of handpicking standards to teach students is how the district wanted math and language arts teachers to prep students for the CAHSEE (although they would never admit to it, but the coercion was there). The fact that so many students could not pass the test—even with everyone having the blueprint to pick and choose what should be taught in the classroom, and some schools went so far as to have a class for students that was just for CAHSEE prep—only goes to demonstrate how teaching to the test is a complete failure.

Just as a reminder, the math portion of the test was at best a reflection of what was taught at the eighth-grade level or earlier. In other words, only some of the math portion of the exam was at the eighth-grade level. The expectations for the English portion were a little more demanding. This part of the test went as high as tenth grade, which was also the first year that the students took the test for the first time.

It is important to understand that the standardized tests themselves should not be blamed. Many people like to blame standardized testing for creating generations of students that are used to short, quick answers and memorizing as opposed to utilizing problem solving skills. There is no doubt whatsoever that standardized testing gave birth to this narrow minded, standards based instruction that has lead us to using pacing guides (as the one you saw earlier) that only focus on certain topics that some people have concluded are important while throwing out others.

It is this picking and choosing of what should be taught in the classroom that has been the reason for the diminishing understanding of mathematics (along with pretty much every other subject). Math is cumulative—as are all the other subjects if you really think about it—a concept learned in the first grade will help create a foundation for understanding of other concepts down the road. But more importantly, if something is missed because RAD decided that it was unimportant for the test and therefore omitted it from a pacing guide, then this will create a Butterfly Effect where the lack of understanding for each subsequent grade level will only increase to the point where the student just decides to give up.

Schools that did well on the CAHSEE were not schools that just taught to the test. They were schools that may have looked at what was on the blueprint, but just kept teaching as they were. Many schools that are successful on these exams are the ones that do not let a small subset of standards dictate how a class is to be taught. The problem is how many administrators, along with some teachers, worship at the altar of these pacing guides generated by someone over at the district office. But as is plainly obvious as it is to everyone but the person putting these guides together, the pacing guide that was shown goes from exponential functions to probability tables in one giant step. This is why so many students have problems when it comes to learning and retaining what they were supposed to have learned in their previous classes.

One of the biggest complaints from teachers (especially math), besides the standard student behavioral issues, is that the students aren't retaining what they are learning in the classroom. Well for one, go back and look at the pacing plan from a few pages ago; there is no way any teacher or administrator should be surprised at how little is retained when all we do is throw a few specific topics at the students and expect them to remember how to do problems related to some specific standard. And believe it or not, some administrators expect the students to memorize (as if they didn't have enough to remember already) the standards that are supposed to be written on the board by the teacher.

When the topics that are taught fluctuate as they do with very little continuity from one to the next, then little or no retention of what was learned should not be surprising to anyone (except RAD of course). Nor should it stun anyone as to why students lose their interest in mathematics, or any other subject, as they continue through their K–12 experience and beyond. Maybe RAD should talk to some actual mathematicians instead of thinking that they know everything about how it is supposed to be taught in the classroom. Math isn't about memorizing a bunch of formulae and regurgitating steps that were shown by someone else to solve a specific type of problem. Unless one has an eidetic memory, it would be impossible to remember everything. But sadly, in many classrooms, this has been and will continue to be the expectation.

Leonard: *Sheldon has kind of a photographic memory.*

Sheldon: *Photographic is a misnomer, I have an eidetic memory as I have told you many times; most recently last year during lunch on the afternoon of May 7th. You had turkey and complained it was dry.*

(The Big Bang Theory)

Granted, it is a little easier than some of the other subjects when it comes to mathematics. Certain definitions such as that of a logarithm or a square root will not change just because some small cohort of people decide what should and should not be taught in the classroom.

So if you teach algebra (or any subject for that matter), or whatever math class it is that you teach, then teach algebra. If you feel that the standards are impeding on your teaching, and more importantly student learning, then just ignore them. But if you are worried about RAD coming in and scrutinizing you for not having some nonsensical piece of Pedagogical Flair on the board, then just do what a colleague of mine did from the social science department: He wrote a standard on one of his whiteboards at the beginning of the year and purposely left it there for the entire semester (might have been the entire year, but I'll have to ask). Regardless, not one of the four administrators (for a student body population of just over one thousand) we had at the time realized this, and it was also marked on his walkthrough results that he had the standards posted for the students to see.

———

It is easier for math than it would be for language arts or the social sciences. Elements of mathematics do not change (please stop using the phrase *new math* by the way... you know who you are). Addition will always be the inverse of subtraction and the third power of two (notice that I didn't say two to the third power) will always be equal to eight; unless you are in some group of numbers mod n where n is less than or equal to eight.

I'm not going to pretend I know the answer for Economics or U.S. History when it comes to standardized testing. The difference for some curricula other than math is that there is quite a bit of memorization when it comes to testing in general. So when it comes to the standards for those types of exams, it is important to know what topics will be covered, but to not use the standards that are given as the only items that are meant to be taught.

As I just mentioned, it is a lot more difficult for those teachers of the social sciences. These classes are obviously more subjective when it comes to drawing a conclusion regarding the outcome of some historical event. The number of events that occurred in the timeline for a U.S. History class is far more than can be taught over a ten-month time frame.

This is where things become problematic; many states are setting their own standards when it comes to teaching the specifics of history be it U.S. or world. This actually makes some sense. Think of it this way: If there were ten people in a room and you were going to order a pizza with exactly two toppings, it is improbable that everyone will agree on what should be on the pizza. So it shouldn't really be a surprise to anyone that there is disagreement from state-to-state regarding which events on a historical timeline merit a place on the list of topics to be taught for those specific classes. Book publishers are also recognizing this and have been writing books specifically for each state and the standards that they choose.

—

For those out there that want to blame standardized testing for this teaching to the test pathway that we have been on for a couple of decades now, it makes sense. After all, standardized testing begat standards based instruction. But this reaction to only teaching specific standards in the classroom based on the exams comes from the pressure that RAD puts on the teachers so as to increase the test scores of the school.

"Don't waste your life following some fool's orders." – Achilles (Troy, 2004)

Clearly, standards based teaching is problematic because many teachers will only focus on certain standards that are set by whoever was paid to create the pacing plans as you saw earlier in the chapter. If a teacher only focuses on just those specific standards and never branches out to make connections with items or concepts that are not on the pacing plan, then many of the students in that particular classroom will simply have a bunch of memorized minutia that might serve them well during a game of Trivial Pursuit.

After being in the system for as long as I have, I can honestly say that the teachers I know whose students have performed well year after year on these standardized exams are also the people that paid the least amount of attention to the standards when it came to teaching their subject. The math teachers that I know whose students always do well are the ones who focus on making the connections between something they are doing in Algebra 2 (just as an example) and something the students did in the first grade. Although I used this example in my last book, I'll use it again for the purpose of demonstration: $\log_4 16 = 2 \to 4^2 = 16$. But $4^2 = 4 \times 4 = 4 + 4 + 4 + 4 = 16$. So once again, the evaluation of a basic logarithmic expression and how it can be taken all the way back to first grade addition.

If it were up to RAD, all students would need to know about the causes of World War I would be the assassination of Archduke Franz Ferdinand and be done with it. Thankfully, I work with some excellent history teachers that will go beyond one or two events that represent a typical academic answer. They will help the students to better understand other issues at the time to give more of a cause and effect perspective. They will discuss other topics that contributed to WWI such as (for example) Imperialism and the amount of tension that was already going on between the Great Powers. And even though making that connection might not be explicitly on the list of standards that they were given, they will do what they can to create a picture for the students that will help them to better comprehend the cause and effect as to how an event of that magnitude takes place.

———

I once worked with another teacher that would always complain about some other teachers on campus (sound familiar?). This teacher's complaint was that other teachers only get the "good students" in their classes. In short, this person was trying to find some rationale as to why his/her students were doing poorly on these EOC exams, whereas some other teachers had students that would always outperform the state average.

If you have ever worked at a school anywhere (or just any job in any industry), you know exactly who this person is that I'm talking about. Regardless of where you teach, there is always that one person that has to find some excuse for their students not doing well. These people will simply not admit that some teachers are just really good at what they do, or perhaps think that the fault lies with them. And instead of trying to maybe learn from these other teacher, they will use the "good students" excuse, along with a long list of others, to try and find fault with the system (or the teachers) that somehow allowed one person to get the good students while they always get the classes full of bad students.

As I mentioned earlier, it has nothing to do with getting the all the good students in a class; some teachers are just excellent at what they do. Yes, there are those teachers (you probably work with a few sycophantic teachers or sycophantic department chairs) that do work out backroom deals with administrators over summer vacation to get a class schedule full of good students—such as honors and AP classes—so as not to have to deal with general students; as their results are usually also mediocre. But I am not talking about these teachers that are part of administration's inner circle. I am talking about teachers that will teach general classes with thirty-plus students in most of their sections. These are people that have anything from multiple sections of algebra to general U.S. History; and yet, year after year, their students have performed well for one reason (and no, it's not because they only get the "good students"). The reason their students do well is that they do not simply teach the standards that are given. Yes, they know what the standards are and they do look at them every now and then, but they do not let them [the standards or RAD] dictate all that is taught in their classroom.

So is standardized testing and therefore standards based teaching going to disappear anytime soon? No, of course it's not. And with Common Core upsetting so many people, it is more than likely that the debate and ire caused by these types of exams are also not going to be ending anytime soon.

As a math teacher and someone with a competitive personality, I enjoy seeing how my students perform (for better or worse) against those at not only other schools in California, but other states as well. And if you are a high school teacher and have proctored the eleventh-grade math test, then you know it is not unfair by any means. Any student in Algebra 2 that paid attention in class should have very little issue when it comes to the exam itself.

So what about those strange homework problems that you see on social media where a parent (who happens to be an engineer) has a son or daughter who didn't receive full credit on a problem for not taking the same approach as the provided rubric in the book? Those types of problems are usually the interpretation of a publisher trying to create types of abstract problems (incorrectly) to show that they are in-the-know when it comes to the Common Core standards. And since these problems will be labeled under some Common Core standard in the book, a teacher will assign them as homework (assuming that the school still gives homework (you might want to look up Wonder, Read, and Play—WRaP)) citing some Common Core standard, and thus the social media rants begin.

There's nothing wrong with using the standards as guidelines, but to only teach those guidelines—which is what administration is pushing more and more for teachers to do—is asinine to say the least; but this is the system as it is for many schools across the country. Teachers are expected to adhere to the standards and only the standards and not to deviate.

As usual, RAD simply does not understand that the idea of standards based learning (obviously some tongue-in-cheek in the chapter title) is not beneficial to those doing the learning. All this has led to, starting from the early grades, are students who are shown certain steps to get a correct answer in lieu of understanding why those steps are correct, or discovering their own rationale to solving whatever problem they are working on for that moment.

- 11 -

Phases of Teaching

The career of teaching can, for the most part, be broken down into three major phases. Each of these individual tiers can be broken down into a number of sub-strata depending on subject matter, personality, response to setbacks (notice I used the plural there, as there will be many) as well as anything else that life outside of the profession throws at someone during their years of teaching, or any career for that matter. And although the individual layers of each phase may be different from one teacher to the next, the overall phases are very generally relatable.

Now before getting into the specifics of the three different phases, these are meant for people who stay in the profession for the majority, if not all, of their adult careers. The people not included are those who, let's say, only see teaching as a stepping-stone on their path toward some project-management position in a corporate office somewhere, quit on the first day, or perhaps don't even make it to the point of having students in a classroom. How might that happen, you ask?

A few years back, a new social science colleague at my site (we use the word "colleague" because we quickly learn not to bother remembering names until we see them on the mailboxes in the staff room) quit before the first day of student attendance. This was during the first week back after summer break when teachers come in to set up their classrooms and prepare for the coming school year. He arrived on Monday to get his keys and to take a look at the classroom he was being assigned of which, having recently been in a credentialing program, he likely saw as the pedagogical space where he would shape the minds of the future. The minds of the present, however, have this little habit of keeping track of which rooms are going to the newbies (who usually only appear as [Sub] on the schedule until after the school-year actually begins, so it's like they don't really exist yet), and scavenging for the resources that, despite the numerous requests for purchase orders or warehouse retrievals, never seem to find their way to the classroom. Thus, he found that much of his furniture was swapped out with old, beat-up desks and chairs, or just missing altogether; the cabinets threadbare and near-broken, and the materials he had planned to use for instilling the love of history in his students having become history themselves. That teacher turned in his keys one day after receiving them and never came back.

Another instance of a person not lasting very long was a math teacher; though he did make it to the first day of students and almost made it through the first day of teaching. But alas, he did not. About half way through the day, he dropped his keys off with the principal's secretary and was also never to be seen or heard from again.

They don't really talk much about this in most credentialing programs, and very often the student-teaching that incoming candidates are made to do can create a few false expectations in terms of what will happen when they have to walk into a classroom and turn it into an imaginative playground of ideas from scratch. They will have to somehow accomplish this using only three rusted cabinets and a roll of crepe-paper that someone was thoughtful enough to dig out of a closet that appears not to have been opened since the mid-seventies. There should be an emoji for the kind of haunted, thousand-yard stare that a teacher has when they're standing in the office ready to turn in their keys after less than a day of teaching, but there are limits to the amount of existential despair you can communicate (although I suspect that RAD is working on an objective rubric for that as part of a Professional Development series that every teacher will be made to attend, or hire someone who is already an "expert" in this for just a few thousand dollars per day).

It's not that teachers are all the same, of course (despite how the complexity and depth of their subject area is treated by administration by being reduced to some set of "teaching strategies" that neglect any content outside of basic communication and note-taking skills), but there are patterns you tend to notice after a while. It usually takes about a decade when you start to really see the hard-bitten countenance of a pre-veteran start to appear... when they start to realize why so much discussion about the teaching profession involves World War I imagery—"in the trenches," "the front lines," "marching orders,"—heck, even the official term for competency is phrased as "fit for duty".

Now that we have that out of the way, let me briefly (I say *briefly* as each individual phase could easily fit into its own tome) discuss each phase of a teacher's career; at least from what I have observed in my near two decades of service.

Phase 1 is what I like to call the *Neophyte* (feel free to use *Newbie* instead). These are the first few golden years when a young, fresh graduate enters the world of pedagogy for the very first time. Understand of course, that the age of a teacher is relative, and it doesn't have to be a young person that just received their college degree—any teaching credential program will require the development of a lofty set of personal standards which will then be slowly eroded by the machine of the education system as the years grind by; no matter the life experience of the person involved. It could easily be someone who left the corporate milieu or some other type of industry, who wanted to dip their toe into the world of teaching and whose first task is figuring out exactly just how deep and potentially scalding those waters are.

"When you're wearing rose-colored glasses, all the red flags just look like flags." – Wanda (Bojack Horseman)

Regardless of age, those first few years of teaching are, for many, quite the clarion call when it comes to the educational industry (yes, I just called it an industry). To be more specific, a producer-subsidized industry... wherein most of the production is dependent on the producer only being vaguely aware of how much they're actually producing. This is what the Neophyte learns during this first stage of pedagogical development that almost certainly will *not* be covered in any of the credential courses (though they will tell you how important it is to italicize or otherwise emphasize the word "not" when writing a multiple choice test).

Neophytes are easy to spot at staff meetings (though they learn to blend in quickly), and can be identified on campus as those who will show up bright-eyed and bushy-tailed, often among the first to arrive, filled with naive thoughts about how they are going to make the changes that will get the students in their classes excited about whatever the subject matter is that they are teaching. They are going to do away with all of the things that they didn't like about school themselves by working with all of the "stakeholders"; from RAD, department chairs, counselors, parents, and students, to anyone else that I may have forgotten to include, of which the sheer numbers become quickly overwhelming when the Neophyte attempts to actually organize such collaboration.

"You are young. Life has been kind to you. You will learn." – Sweeny Todd (Sweeny Todd: The Demon Barber of Fleet Street, 2007)

Some figure it out quicker than others, but the influence that one person can have on a system of interaction that includes all the "stakeholders" might not be as large as they'd hoped, and the effort necessary for, say, ensuring that studying happens for each student at home to some degree, or perhaps communicating the importance of one's subject to a doubtful parent, or maybe explaining to a student that hitting someone in the face during class is a poor form of conflict resolution, is exponentially larger than they had anticipated. The dreams Neophytes enter the field with can be disillusioned pretty quickly without the support of administration or a trusted veteran to work with to help them through each day; who understands that the flowcharts of contact-points and lists of help-lines are much more theoretical than that on which can be depended upon to be timely, or often even remotely useful.

The Neophyte's bad dreams can become nightmares if and when one particular administrator does not like them for whatever reason, and they begin to suspect (all-too-often and with good reason) that there is a very high probability, regardless of how effective a new teacher may be in the classroom, that they will not be returning for the next school year.

This is another reality-check when first starting out as a teacher. The fact is that if one administrator does not like you for whatever the reason, regardless as to whether or not that administrator is also your evaluator, it is very likely—since the new teacher is at the bottom of the seniority list and doesn't have tenure—that the new teacher will simply not be re-elected to the position. But it doesn't have to be an administrator who doesn't like the new teacher for them to be let go in March (the month that pink slips usually go out; which English and History teachers are fond to point out often falls on the 15th—beware the Ides, Neophyte...). A new teacher could simply rub a veteran teacher who is in an administrator's trusted inner-circle the wrong way; that might also be enough to let the Neophyte go as well. As I've mentioned, it could have very little to do with how effective (or ineffective) the new teacher is with their students and much more to do with qualities of a more personal, political, or ideological nature (since it really is the same old game of the office-popularity contest that it's been since "Welcome Back Kotter" in all too many ways).

In addition to the possibility of not getting along with RAD, there is also the realization that, as a teacher, you are very likely to be evaluated by someone who knows very little about your subject matter. They are the ones that tell a teacher whether or not they are doing a good job with the students. Think about that for a second: A former PE teacher could be the evaluator for someone teaching AP Physics or AP Chemistry. Just kind of sit back and think about that one for a few minutes. There are also many instances where the observer has little or no teaching experience at the level of the teachers that he or she is observing and evaluating. While this is usually something discussed to some (however little) degree in a decent credentialing program, the Neophyte could not possibly be prepared for the cognitive dissonance necessary to process an evaluation meeting where someone who literally does not have the most basic understanding of the subject that they've [the teacher] devoted an entire career to fostering and developing their own perspective of a subject. Regardless, their evaluator will stare them dead in the eyes and try to explain that they need to break down their information into more "chunkable" bits so that students can "chew" them in a more objectively testable way. When that subject is English, it can be even more disheartening (I've heard tell of a Neophyte having to explain what the word "cinematic" meant to his evaluator, who was a VP from elementary who had decided to take a job at the high school level).

———

I recall one faculty meeting many years ago, where one of the new teachers spoke up about the lack of discipline at the school. This person was, as any new teacher complaining about discipline would have to be, throwing stones in a glass house in terms of their own classroom management—but they definitely put in the best effort that they could, and considering that the game of *dangling multiple candidates over one position for so long while waiting until the last second to hire someone* usually leaves the selection pool a little empty, as most will take other jobs by the time the district decides to make the offer, I thought they were at least better than average.

I remember looking at the people sitting at the same table I was, and all of us had the same, hard-bitten expression on our face which essentially added up to: *this person will not be coming back next year.* It was like we were watching a gladiator match and all mentally pointing our thumbs the same way, having seen how the bluster of overconfidence has felled greater warriors than this before... And wouldn't you know it, that very person who complained about the lack of discipline (and deservedly so) was not re-elected for the next school year.

The replacement was much worse, naturally, because they dangled the position for so long the resultant selection pool was lackluster at best... if only someone noticed this pattern... well, plenty of us have, just not those in charge of doing the hiring.

In short, if you are a Neophyte and want to keep your job, then either agree with what administration is saying regardless of how asinine or incongruous their ramblings might sound, and tell them how amazing their ideas are; or just simply sit there, stay put, and don't say anything at all—especially if it is in contradiction to yet another progressive, paradigm-shifting idea from RAD or one of their inner-circle sycophants.

"Mr. Madison, what you just said is one of the most insanely, idiotic things I have ever heard. At no point in your rambling, incoherent response were you even close to anything that could be considered a rational thought." – James Downey (Billy Madison, 1995) / The Inner-Thoughts of a teacher at any phase during any given RAD-sermon about almost anything of practical relevance; be it during a Professional Development Seminar or evaluation meeting.

And since you are a newbie (they literally use the term "beginning teacher" in most districts, but it really does just mean N00B, if you're semi-fluent in gamerspeak) and will have the status of Probationary Teacher for at least the first two years... do not, and I repeat, do *not* (remember what you learned about emphasizing that word? It applies, since your entire probationary period is a giant test the likes of which might only be compared to the Kobayashi-Maru) say or do anything that might upset your evaluator. You could be an English teacher who has all of your students reading *Crime And Punishment* and discussing the comic relief that Razumihin brings to the story, and if whoever your evaluator is does not like you, then you will not only receive a notice of non re-elect, but you will now have a bad evaluation on your record that will go with you to your next job interview (though the sheer absurdity of teaching fantastic realism while so obviously living in it does provide some existential relief).

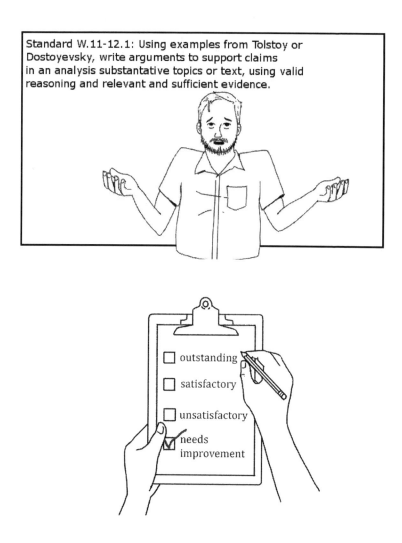

Standard W.11-12.1: Using examples from Tolstoy or Dostoyevsky, write arguments to support claims in an analysis substantive topics or text, using valid reasoning and relevant and sufficient evidence.

☐ outstanding

☐ satisfactory

☐ unsatisfactory

☑ needs improvement

Now, if a Neophyte has any semblance of integrity (which it's not recommended that you openly display until you obtain tenure), and expects students to earn their grades as opposed to just giving a grade to appease RAD, and are willing to report a failing grade for a student who does not live up to the basic expectations of what you would consider necessary for any class, such as just showing up on a fairly regular basis, turning in homework on time, and understanding that plagiarism is not acceptable, then they are in for a very difficult thirty-year stint in the education system.

Obviously, there is some tongue-in-cheek in that last paragraph—along with the rest of this book as well as the previous book, as well as in the voice of anyone who might hope to retire from a career in Education—but if a Neophyte gives a student an F on a plagiarized assignment, or if the student is in an honors or AP course and the same teacher tries to drop the student because of the infraction, then that N00B might be in for a rude awakening, because they don't really understand the rules of the game yet.

Depending on the school district and site administration, it is very likely that it will be determined by the administrative team whose job it is to confer the most prudent academic decision to be the fault of the teacher for giving too much work, or perhaps assigning a task that required more than ten minutes of effort; which is why the student copied or just didn't do that assignment to begin with, but which will be described as "failing to adequately adapt the curriculum to meet identified student needs" (also known as "differentiating instruction"), and which will be blamed on the lack of professional experience in terms of how recently this educator has been in the profession.

Understand that I am not talking about a second or third-grade student who might not understand exactly what plagiarism means. I am talking about the middle school or high school student that has been around long enough to know that this behavior is, or at least should be, unacceptable. This, of course, is not always the case.

—

A friend of mine teaches an AP U.S. History class and holds his students accountable to the contract that they receive at the end of the school year that precedes the year that they will be enrolled in the class along with their summer assignment. The students are required to read, sign, and turn it in to the teacher at the beginning of the school year once they return in August. Parts of the contract include but are not limited to: completing homework assignments, coming to class prepared, attending tutoring, and a part about academic integrity and how plagiarism will not be tolerated.

As most teachers, or nearly close to all now, he does have the occasional issue of a student copying work off the internet. The first time this happens with a particular student, he will be nice about it and gives any student who admits to the infraction a second chance. It is an extremely rare case that a student does this twice in his AP class (general classes are a completely different matter).

The majority of those caught will admit to doing so and are given the opportunity to stay in the class. The ones that deny it (even with proof) are removed immediately (or as immediately as possible, pending parent meetings with a counselor and administrator). It must also be taken into consideration that if these students who do copy and turn in work as their own original document, and do so as comfortably as they do, then it is more than likely they have been getting away with plagiarizing for more than just this one instance.

One particular student was caught this year and given the same warning that is given to all of the students in this teacher's class. And like so many high school students reason (and plenty of adults in the workplace, for that matter), if they get away with it once, why not do it again? Shortly after he was caught the first time, he submitted plagiarized work for a second time.

The teacher, however, was not willing to deal with the plagiarism this time around. He emailed the counselor and told him the issue with the student and that he is to be removed from the AP class. Yes, you know very well which way this is going. Here is part of the response (as is) from the student's counselor regarding the plagiarized assignment: *"He did mentioned that he had difficulty with an essay and DBQ, thus he used the internet to copy work."*

This counselor was trying to defend the student copying work because of the difficulty of the assignment... even though it was a direct violation of the contract (not to mention the student handbook that all students receive at the beginning of the year) that the student signed, and it was his second instance for this specific AP class. Although the student was eventually removed from the class, the fact that the student was getting support and defense from a counselor (no, this wasn't the first time and it won't be the last) is one reason so many students think that there are little or no consequences for their actions.

I know of another teacher who had a sophomore English Honors class for which a student simply stopped showing up for two weeks (which happened to be near the end of the quarter and thus particularly crucial). When they were dropped, and wanted to re-enroll, the teacher met with the parents and counselor and simply said, "It's clear that the student has made his choice here, and they are not interested in the honors curriculum. They may still take a college-prep course (another name for a general English class). They have missed too much material to be able to reasonably continue in the course". Later, after that student had been transferred to the other Honors English course (through a rearrangement of his class schedule), he [the teacher] casually mentioned to the counselor that he had feared he may have sort of come off as an a-hole, and the counselor simply responded with, "No—what you don't understand is that I had promised you'd let him back in, and you made *me* look like the a-hole"! This is when he realized he was a Neophyte, however, and didn't understand that the fact that these parents were either going to have their child enrolled in an honors class, or find an equally competitive school (there's one not far; a newly opened school with only 10th grade students) in which he would be placed without question, made their patronage as consumers of the education industry among the top priority.

———

Taking a side step for just a minute; the teachers that I am referring to here are not ones that sit around and press the play button for a living. They are not the ones that take the easy way out and just give A's and B's to appease the almighty RAD. These are also the teachers that open themselves up to scrutiny from administration because they make their students earn their grades instead of just giving them away. These are people that hold their students to high standards and, even more importantly, themselves.

Let us not forget that the greatest insult of "No Child Left Behind" (NCLB) was that the state would have standards that are higher than those who devote their careers to an industry that prides itself on the self-sacrifice of the teachers who define it. Neophytes now-a-days may not remember, but there was a time when it was assumed that anyone willing to go into such an industry were clearly committed to whatever degree of confidence they had in the nobility of their pursuit, since teaching was never a career that promised anything but the meagerest of material wealth... but that was before the crash of 2008, so... [awkwardly backs out of room].

Teachers, regardless of their current phase, are constantly

finding themselves in defense mode when it comes to actions of students such as plagiarism, or even a student using profanity in a threatening fashion towards a teacher. More often than not, the teacher will have to defend himself or herself in front of a parent, counselor, and administrator as to why, as in the case of the plagiarism, the student took the action that they did. Often, the teacher will be put at fault and the action of the student in question will be re-designated as a reaction to that of the teacher's action. In other words, the student plagiarized because the teacher put him into a situation where doing so was the only solution.

Now for emphasis, this was only one AP student who already had one warning about turning in work that was copied off of the internet. But this act of simply copying and pasting work and turning it in for credit is almost the norm. Some students will actually submit work that has been copied and pasted from the internet with the hyperlinks to different websites still underlined and not give it a second thought as to why this is just not acceptable.

More often than not, a Neophyte (or any teacher for that matter, but especially the newbie) will have to sit with what essentially amounts to a jury that has already made up their mind on who the guilty party is; having to defend their actions as if they were the ones who did something wrong is definitely something that they do not cover in the teacher credentialing classes. It's this type of event which, to say the least, is somewhat disheartening when a new-to-the-system teacher first comes to the realization that they aren't in Kansas anymore.

So for those of you teaching college classes and also have an increase in the number of students that turn in plagiarized work and don't seem to understand why doing so is wrong and merits a failing grade for the assignment, then look no further than those who constantly enabled those students and the school districts from whence they came.

—

It is usually towards the end of stage one or the beginning of stage two (depending on the person), where the teacher will start to realize that the system does not care about their ideas nor how effective they are in the classroom. If they figure this out early enough, they will also come to the conclusion that there are some teachers (you know who they are) who do not work nearly as hard as they do and also do very little when it comes to getting their paychecks. Most eye-opening is that instance when a Neophyte realizes that these are the same teachers who could easily be making double their salary simply because of the number of years served as well as possibly having one of those worthless (when it comes to actual teaching) master's degrees in education.

Just in case you were wondering, the majority of K–12 teachers that have a master's degree have it in the field of education. The reason is that it is very easy to earn get one of these, as just about all of the course work can be done online in a very short amount of time without a lot of accountability (compared to the scrutiny of an incoming teacher, it's almost completely absent of oversight). And yet, when it comes to the classroom, it offers little (if anything) as it pertains to the effectiveness of a teacher. If you were to ask the holders of these degrees, many will openly admit that they did it simply for the money; almost all school districts require a master's degree as the only way to get to that last column of pay for a teacher (not to mention the secret doctoral pay-scale that exists like the hidden In-N-Out menu... ask around).

This is another let-down moment when a new teacher

realizes that the system values them financially by the number of years served as opposed to their productivity in the classroom. Even more demoralizing than the financial aspects based on years of service, is the fact that the system does not value them at all when it comes to what they are being paid to do.

For a more personalized first person account that demonstrates how little the system cares about the efficacy of a teacher, and how it easily it can break a Neophyte, please read Chris' Story; which is the last chapter of *The Need For Common Core*.

Many Neophytes will go from job to job those first few years simply because there might have been an administrator who did not like something they did in the classroom. All the while that teacher pressing the play button for twenty years sits back in their chair, puts their feet up on their desk and, as long as they stay within the district, can cruise their way to retirement.

———

Most Neophytes usually learn pretty quickly that a thick skin is needed to survive in education. Many are simply dumbfounded when they come to the conclusion that the problems of a teacher usually have very little to do with the actual act of teaching. And if that thick skin does not develop quickly (if at all) then this person will either not get to the second phase of teaching, or if they decide to stick it out, are in for a very rough, thirty-year ride.

"Listen, Colonel, um... Sherman. You can give me 100 good reasons to leave, and I can't give you one good reason to stay— stay anyway." – Benjamin Franklin 'Hawkeye' Pierce (MASH)

It's at this point that most Neophytes move into the second

stage of teaching: *Surviving.*

Before getting into Phase 2, the reason I wrote *most* Neophytes in the last paragraph is because there are a few sycophants in education that always have it easy. The reason for this is because of their weathervane mentality that will blow in the direction of the ideologies of whoever is currently sitting in the administrative offices. The personality of these teachers will mold around the current boss is in order to gain access to the inner circle. They are able to set aside their pride and integrity—then again maybe they just don't have any to begin with—in order to curry the favor of site and district office administration in the hopes that reciprocation will be the end result.

This act of ass-kissing is usually rewarded with praise and a nice teaching schedule regardless of how effective the teacher may or may not be. An absolutely awful teacher will constantly be praised by RAD in emails and faculty meetings if the teacher does a good enough job of ingratiating themselves to those who they feel matter the most. And what of the other teachers who show up and do an excellent job where it counts? Well, as long as they don't speak up against administration, they will be left alone. But once you start questioning RAD and any decisions that they feel are best for the school regardless as to whether or not they [the decision] actually are, then you, my friend, better be ready to have a big target placed on your back. The good news is, however, with today's administrative turnover rate, it's very unlikely that the target will be on your back for more than three years; though based on personal experience, it will be a pretty grueling three years.

As I mentioned a little earlier, it is important to note that the three phases are not equal in length. For the most part, the Neophyte stage is usually the shortest. The last two will vary depending on how many rounds a teacher can go with the never ending deluge of revolving door administrators that set foot on campus. The problem with putting up a fight is that the people with whom the teacher is fighting against changes every two to three years. This makes it even tougher because you end up going into battle all over again with a new set of administrators who have similar ideologies as those who just left.

———

But it's not just administrators, as you previously read. Counselors (not all, but in my experience about a third) will often side with the parent and the student. The reason for this being that a student will frequent the counselor's office and tell them how bad teacher x and teacher y are at teaching which is why they are not doing well in the class. Many will simply take the sob-story of the student as truth (without first doing some due diligence and checking the history of the student), and console them to let him or her know that it's not their fault that they are doing poorly in the class, but that of the teachers.

Taking a side step for just a moment; I'm not talking about those students who put forth an effort and occasionally have an issue with a teacher that will result in a conference to try and workout what the problems might be. I'm referring to those students who have a history of ditching class, and when they do show up, they are never prepared and are also disruptive to the learning process of the other thirty-plus students in the class. These are the students that will just walk around the school and be told nothing by administration when they are passed in the hallway. These are the students that have been caught plagiarizing, ditching, using and selling drugs, as well as a number of other items that are in their file. And yet, even though these students might attend their classes maybe half of the time, the teacher will somehow be blamed for the students failing.

Imagine getting into a boxing ring against an opponent for two or three rounds, then getting a new opponent to fight because the first one decided to leave for another higher paying boxing ring down the road. To make it worse, some rounds will give you multiple foes, be they counselors, other teachers, parents, guardians, or anyone else that I may have forgotten about to go up against (this is the point at which the teacher realizes that the "stakeholders" are all holding actual stakes...). Add to that the revolving door administration as it currently is, and the opponents will not stop until the teacher quits, retires, or simply gives in to the pressure and becomes the wet-rag of having-a-pulse-confers-passing-mentality simply because they really do not feel like fighting the same fight anymore.

It is important to understand that *Surviving* doesn't mean that the teacher is solely worried about keeping their job. It's about trying to keep your standards high in your classroom and holding one's self and students accountable, all the while not giving in to the pressures from all around to just pass students in order to keep the graduation rate in an uptrend. It's about coming up with the energy to go to another parent-teacher-counselor-administrator meeting knowing there is a high likelihood that the blame for all the problems will somehow be placed on you and your actions.

There is the anecdote of a teacher who was accused of discriminating against a student because her sister was a lesbian... when this teacher didn't even know that a) they were sisters, or b) that she was a lesbian. Nevertheless, the VPs and counselors couldn't bring themselves to say that the accusation was absurd because to do so would be invalidating the perspective of the student, which is the only thing you can never do as anyone who realizes that the students are the consumers, ultimately, in this producer-based industry of education, and their emotional barometers as communicated to their parents, given a sufficient amount of choice in which educational options those parents have in terms of school choice, will determine the degree to which it is expected that the teacher defer to the experience of student-discomfort by adjusting the parameters to which that student might be considered to be "passing".

This is the subtext of every meeting you will ever have as a teacher, and you learn to just realize that the counselors are usually more aware of the socio-cultural politics that confer value on parents because they have better sources of information, and you try to figure out how much pushback to give based on what they seem to communicate is likely to be possible in the first place. That's how you survive: You slowly accept the immutable sociopolitical structure of the district in which you have been hired, and which usually only happens long after you realize that to abandon ship at this point would result in lost years of seniority, or a straight pay-cut; as many school districts do not accept all the years of service when a teacher goes from one school district to another. These are the hard-line economic decisions that shouldn't apply to the noble profession of education... but which very much do.

Surviving is about maintaining that piece of you that is slowly being chiseled away by a system that does not care how effective or ineffective a person is in the classroom.

"They send you here for life, that's exactly what they take; the part that counts, anyways." – Red (The Shawshank Redemption, 1994)

Backtracking for just a moment, not all parent-teacher-counselor-administrator meetings are like that as just described. There are occasionally those parents who, because they have been involved in their child's education (especially if they have been in the same district the entire time, as rare as that seems to be in many areas) understand that it isn't the fault of the teacher; especially if they know the teacher from previous years. But when it comes down to the tone of a meeting, it is the parents that dictate the direction. And the more of these types of meetings that a teacher goes through where they find that they are in defense mode, a little bit more of the part that counts is removed until eventually there is very little left for the system to chisel away. After long enough, it becomes clear that the trope of the teacher "who just doesn't understand what it takes" will be projected exactly as hard as is necessary to wear down a teacher enough to get them to give into whatever demands are being put forth. When you have that particular wool pulled out from under you (I have seen more than my fair share of these situations; both as the teacher in question as well as many colleagues), you tend to stop pretending you can be a Neophyte anymore. That's when you get Destiny's Child with it and become a Survivor.

———

For most teachers (or just the majority of people in general), the last thing they want to do is look back on a career spanning, in many cases, thirty-plus years and come to the conclusion that the time spent in the classroom was simply squandered. This is also the time in a teacher's life that they start to really question the choice of going into teaching in the first place. It's that junction of a teacher's life where they aren't too old to go to another district, or to reinvent themselves and leave the teaching profession to try a different career. At the same time, they are also at that point where they feel dependent on the system that they have been part of for the majority of their life.

There is also that feeling that leaving a school district, after serving for so many years, for another district would mean starting all over at the bottom rung of the seniority ladder and having to climb it all over again. That's partly because literally after about five years in any district, there are financial penalties one would have to suffer from transferring districts, be it either from the inequality of year-to-year-transfer in terms of accepted time toward retirement, or from the fact that entrance into a new district enables them to the vulnerability of not having tenure, and also subjects them to the same two-year crap-shoot (do I get along with these people?) as they had when they took their first teaching job. But this time around they are not some young twenty-something fresh out of college still looking to take those first steps after finishing one side of the educational coin.

It is also at this point that many simply do not want to leave so as to not feel like a quitter. There still exists that naive part of them (still a Neophyte at heart) that wants to believe the promises that administration makes to the staff about how next year is going to somehow be better; though it rarely, if ever, is actually better.

This is also the phase of a teacher's life where many of them are now responsible for more than just themselves. Most will now have a couple of kids, possibly a mortgage, maybe taking care of a parent, and any other aspects of life that may have not existed during the Neophyte stage. Let's face it: The idea of teaching as a public profession that might allow one to raise a family on a single income is pretty deeply-ingrained into the American consciousness, if such a thing exists. And the actual ability of that happening seems to be evaporating like that chem-teacher's realization that the resources just ain't there, and they either have to double-down into a place they never asked to be, but which is better than nothing, or keep hunting for that Shangri-La of a district that truly values them. And as you probably know, that uncertainty of wanting to start over at a new school or just a different profession in general, can be a bit unnerving as other facets of life begin to take precedent.

"Oh, god, that would be an adventure. But no, no, I'm a husband and a father, I have responsibilities. Life can't be all pleasure and distraction." – Stede Bonnet (Assassin's Creed 4: Black Flag, 2013)

This takes us to the last phase of teaching: *Capitulation.* This is the third and final stage that all teachers at some point will get to; some will get there much sooner than others. For some, Capitulation might occur fifteen years before retirement, and for others, it may just be a few weeks before turning in their keys for one last time. It's sort of like enlightenment in a vague Buddhist sense... that moment where you realize your fate is sealed and you don't really have any other choice but to keep going because there's really no other road left to travel (unless one is willing to go into administration).

Capitulation usually occurs after a teacher has taken on too many battles and really doesn't feel like fighting anymore. It's that point late enough in their career that they know there is no way for them to be let go because of their place on the seniority list—barring some sort of incident involving physical contact or some type of misconduct that could lead to them to being fired. They would just prefer to cruise through those last few years into retirement and be done with the system, and prefer to stay out of as many battles as possible with whatever RAD that is currently at their site—and believe me when I say they will have seen many throughout their career. Don't get me wrong here, Capitulation is not the same thing as giving up; they still try to reach as many students as they can and still continue to put forth their best efforts. But it's really more about knowing who your audience really is, and recognizing that the amount of people who realize what you're trying to do is somewhat limited.

—

I have oftentimes heard from a parent, student, co-worker, or someone not in education for that matter, when the topic comes up about a teacher who conveys the appearance that he or she simply does not care anymore. My response is usually along the lines that it isn't that these people don't care, it's just that the system has a way of taking that part of the person that turned this once *Neophyte* into the person who has that appearance that they simply do not care; though I can assure you that they still do... well at least most of them. They try to continue to do so, but usually that means standing up for what they believe as a person and, as so often is the case, what an individual teacher believes and what RAD believes have a tendency to be mutually exclusive, leading to yet another battle in which the authority of rank will be questioned... and as long as the hierarchy of education is based upon theory more than practice, then the one who has managed to appear more educated will reign above the one with the experience to know what complications exist for which no education can prepare one for.

The problem is that one who has reached this stage of teaching has gone head-to-head with so many revolving door administrators, enabling parents, placated students, co-workers, and anyone else I forgot to mention, that it just doesn't seem worth it, as the outcome will rarely, if ever, result in any sort of change that will improve the system, nor will it be different from the outcomes of years past, as evidence from a continued awareness of years that have accumulated. It is at this spot that one looks back from a projected twenty-five, thirty, or even forty years and realizes that when it comes to the battles that have been fought throughout them, the number in the wins column is much less than the number in the loss column, if their experience so far is any guide in terms of how likely the future will be. And for emphasis, many of these conflicts are against a different set of people over similar issues which really aid in wearing down the part of the person that came into this profession so many years earlier.

"Time passes. As we get older, things seem less important." – Ivan (RED, 2010)

Understand that the Capitulation phase does not mean that the teacher shows up every day, sits in his or her chair, and presses the play button (although there are those who do reach that extreme stage) knowing full well that there is nothing that can be done to them when they take this course of action. I personally know many teachers who have reached this phase and still do an excellent job where it counts: the classroom. They have not given up on their students or the job that they are being paid to do. They still work hard as they always have, but have one less of a weight on their shoulders, which also just happens to be the biggest weight of all in the form of a revolving door administrator.

I want to stress that the Capitulation phase isn't meant to be negative. A teacher in this third and final phase simply does not want to make anymore waves, or find themselves in yet another meeting having to defend one's self yet again for a similar set of circumstances that they have seen so many times before, but in front a different set of people. As someone currently in the Survival stage, I can assure that the cases of déjà vu increase quite a bit as the years pass.

This is the phase where a teacher realizes that it is very

unlikely that one can re-invent themselves outside of the educational system. It is at this point they realize that the only other option (as some will take in order to get more money for retirement, we begin to realize as the harrowing monkey's-paw of an alternative) is to take that giant leap into administration. With the simplicity of getting an administrative credential, it is not uncommon for a teacher to spend their last three or four years as an administrator knowing full-well that even if the leap doesn't work out, they could always just go back to the classroom or retire. Finding work as an administrator knowing that a comfortable retirement is all but certain is not very difficult. They all know in the back of their mind that even just one year of administrative pay will add a nice income increase to their golden years.

But for the majority of those that stay in the classroom, these are the final years of a long career that—when looking back—went by in the blink of an eye. This is when they decide to color within the lines and really just try to stay out of the way of RAD, and let the *Neophytes* and *Survivors* take on the battles that they have been part of so many times. Eventually, you realize that there are no more battles to be fought, except for the ones of which you are a willing participant.

"But I'm telling you these walls are funny. First you hate 'em, then you get used to 'em. Enough time passes, you get so you depend on them. That's institutionalized." – Red (The Shawshank Redemption, 1994)

Please don't draw the wrong picture of someone who has capitulated, especially in the sense of the picture in the back of the book (based on multiple true stories by the way). They do not walk into work hunched over with their head hanging down in the admission of defeat. In fact, it's probably just the opposite of that. With RAD rarely on their case about anything, because they are staying within the lines, they have a lot less to worry about when they go home at night; such as an up-and-coming meeting with RAD as to why you told your students that college isn't the only available option after high school. There is also no longer that worry and anxiety of stressing over the evaluation process from an administrator that might know absolutely nothing about their subject. A teacher with only four years (just as an example) left before retirement will only have to go through the evaluation process maybe two more times before they retire, and the outcomes of those evaluations are all but meaningless.

Those who have capitulated have a lot less weight on their shoulders when they come into work every day. It's those in the first two stages that walk in hunched over with their head hanging low (metaphorically speaking... but not really) and holding on to their beloved spoon. Trudging into work wondering what nonsensical piece of pedagogical policy RAD will throw at them and expect them to immediately implement (along with everything else that has been put forth), regardless of how asinine the new faux panacea will be (don't forget: it *will* shift your paradigm).

The teachers who have reached this third and final stage will just go with the flow and ask very little, if any, questions at all. Those of us still yet in the first two stages will question RAD of the value of whatever the new policy is—only to be met with another round of incongruous answers. And it's very difficult to argue against someone who doesn't understand the policy that they are in support of, and can't come up with their own cogent argument as to why they support it (though they will use the line, "The studies have shown that... "). Is it just me, or does this sound a lot like administrative support and the complete misunderstanding of the PBIS construct? There's a certain déjà vu happening here...

For many, especially as it gets late in the game with respect to their career, it is just easier to ride the waves and nod one's head in agreement instead of questioning the validity, effectiveness, or cost of whatever new policy (which is the same as the old policy, but with a different name, spin, and inevitable acronym) is presently being forced upon them.

"The only thing we can do is make what happens in between, count." – Jade Aldemir (Dying Light, 2015)

There simply appears to be a dividing line between those who can determine the thanks of those they have actually educated, and the thanks of a system that rewards those who can demonstrate evidence of such a thing. If you don't know the difference... you might just be a RAD. And if your first instinct is to defer to a chart instead of an actual interaction with an actual student... well, you're probably almost definitely a RAD. We don't blame you, really. After all, you are simply taking advantage of the glitches in a system in the same fashion that students do when trying to find the easiest way to graduation.

People really shouldn't be too surprised at the quality of many of these Nouveau Administrators when teachers that are still in the Neophyte stage and are nowhere near a seasoned veteran, who are still trying to figure out how to teach their own subject (though their selective memory once they become an administrator will be that every day was a pedagogical masterpiece), who still do not fully understand how to use the student information system, are allowed to become an administrator of a school.

When all is said and done, many teachers (irrespective of which of the three phases of teaching that they currently reside) simply want to make a difference in the lives of those that they are here to help. And even though their own perception of the job will change many times throughout the course of their career, the majority of them—with the exception of those who show up and fall asleep while their students are watching yet another video—will fight and try to win as many battles as possible knowing that the war will continue long after they walk out of their classroom one last time. They will try to accomplish as much as they can and help all those who will accept their help for what is considered by many to be a thankless job.

- 12 -

Ensuing Insanity

If you were to draw a representation of school districts as a person, with the relative amounts of power being shown by respective size of bodily appendages, its cranium would not be the largest part of its body... it would be the hands. Greasing palms and buddy-buddying among those who you see as part of the same group is pretty much how every system is run. When it comes to education, districts are being run by a top-heavy set of administrators that make the decisions—along with the local board of education—that dictate all of the rules and regulations that the sites within the district must follow.

"The distinguishing mark of man is the hand, the instrument with which he does all his mischief." – George Orwell (Animal Farm)

Essentially, this means that the promise of an easily-implementable program (many admin still refer to this as "paradigm shifting") that merely requires the application of a system of telling other people what to do; it's a brilliant marketing move for whoever pitches it to the people who use money to tell other people what to do. The rub is that the administrators making and approving the purchases usually have no idea what they're being used for, but they will make the purchase anyways as they need to show that they are being proactive when it comes to student learning, and purchasing things is one means for administration to demonstrate they are doing just that. It's this act of blindly buying into some flavor of the month acronym that demonstrates a major problem of education. One of the reasons why the promise of throwing money at the problems is so misguided is that it's just enabling the attempt to buy our way out of having attempted to have electronic gadgets solve our problems for us. Hence, for those of you thinking or hoping that some sort of dramatic change is coming soon to a school district near you (with the exception of the state taking over an entire district), this is about as likely as RAD coming to the realization that throwing more technology at students isn't going to fix the problems of the education system.

The things that administration thinks are needed to make a school system better are actually making it worse. But they [RAD et al.] are too narrow-minded to understand that what they are trying to do is simply not working. Recognizing this would, of course, violate the central premise that they might be required to implement some nebulously defined "piece" [listen for this term, if you're a teacher in 2018... it's on the rise] of the overall implementation plan that relates to the ESLRs (Expected Schoolwide Learning Results) which fulfill the WASC (Western Association of Schools and Colleges) recommendations that might raise the projected KPI (Key Performance Indicators); the new API (Annual Performance Index) for CC (Common Core) testing. Not only is it not working, but in their mind they think that it is; which only exacerbates the situation. The typical response when something that was paid for doesn't work as planned is that admin will just continue to throw money at it until either some benefits are found, or they leave for a different job at another district because they *literally think that people just weren't good enough at following their directions,* as opposed to considering that what it was that they purchased might not have been the best thing for the school.

Regardless if you think the system is working or not—the latter being the apparent consensus (provided that you assess the success of education as the ability to produce autonomous, free-willed, and informed people who have equal access to information and ability to interpret it; I don't know, you might differ as to your own personal interpretation, but that would require the free will to interpret information, so it's sort of a sticky wicket, right?), this is the way it is going to be for the majority of school districts across the country ad infinitum. The people at the top are going to be the ones making the decisions with very little input (especially when it comes to lower performing, inner city schools), if any, from those that said decisions affect the most.

"But they are the gatekeepers. They are guarding all the doors they are holding all the keys, which means that sooner or later someone is going to have to fight them." – Morpheus (The Matrix, 1999)

So what is it that allows a small handful of individuals to make decisions such as what classes a school offers to its students or how the received monies are spent? Is it decades of classroom experience? No, in fact for most states all it takes is two (three in some states with "higher standards"—sarcasm intended) years of teaching experience to become an administrator. Then it must be experience at multiple levels of teaching, right? Sadly, that would also be a *no*. Most administrators have taught at one level (such as middle school) for all of their classroom experience and, more often than not, get an administrative job at a different level than that which they taught. Surely, you say, then it must be years of studying different types of curricula both past and present and how they relate to the modern day student... no? *"No... and don't call me Shirley"* – Dr. Rumack (Airplane!, 1980). None of those just mentioned represent a pre-requisite to becoming an administrator at a school site or a district office.

So then what separates those who run a school district from those who are subject to playing by their sets of rules? As usual, when it comes to any bureaucratic mess, just some pieces of paper are all that is needed for a person to become an administrator. In the case of education, that would amount to an administrative credential and a master's degree in education; neither of which do anything to help those at the top to be more effective at running the sites within a school district or the district office itself. If anything, these pieces of paper are why more districts ~~seem to be~~ are definitely moving in the wrong direction. Not only do these pieces of paper not help a person to be any more effective than they were as a teacher, but it also instills upon them an increase of hubris that those of us in the classroom now have to deal with.

"You dropped a hundred and fifty grand on a f#ck!n' education you could have gotten for a dollar fifty in late charges at the public library." – Will Hunting (Good Will Hunting, 1997)

You knew that was coming at some point.

Just to reiterate what I wrote previously; a master's degree in education is usually just a few more classes after the teaching credential (depending on whether or not you go back to school years later as opposed to taking a combo curriculum which many new teachers do in order to get both at once). Many education programs are now advertised as a "credential and master's degree hybrid curriculum" where soon-to-be teachers are able to work on both concurrently. Universities really need to stop calling it a "master's" in education, as it really does nothing to help those receiving it to really master anything, with the exception of understanding that getting one (usually through a for-profit college) will move them over at least one column when it comes to placement on the salary schedule.

Perhaps you might think that getting one of these degrees would require the person to take a more advanced and challenging curriculum much like anyone who has a master's degree in any other subject matter besides education. In other words, if a person were to get a master's degree in chemistry, it wouldn't be a few more online classes after they have obtained their degree in chemistry.

Yet, these people that take less challenging classes to get their master's degree in education are the ones that eventually make the leap into administration. The last step would simply be to take a year of online courses to get that administrative credential. And with more would-be teachers taking the hybrid teaching credential/master's in education programs that are pretty much the norm, the more Nouveau Administrators we will be getting as these are the same people that will be adding an administrative credential to their list of qualifications on their résumé.

The people that I know with a master's degree outside of education took multiple years in order to earn it. I do not know of one person that earned it in less than two years and, for most of them, it took at least three years to complete. It is also not unheard of (with the exception of education and maybe a small group of others) for people to take five or six years to complete a *real* master's degree program.

Because when it comes to what a *real* teaching degree would look like in terms of terminality, one must admit that it is either a PhD or MFA... because whether you see it as a philosophy or an art, teaching is not something that can be applied like a programmer applying various algorithms to its data set—or have we so soon forgotten the lesson of Mr. M'Choakumchild?

"NOW, what I want is, Facts. Teach these boys and girls nothing but Facts. Facts alone are wanted in life. Plant nothing else, and root out everything else. You can only form the minds of reasoning animals upon Facts: nothing else will ever be of any service to them. This is the principle on which I bring up my own children, and this is the principle on which I bring up these children. Stick to Facts, sir!" – Mr. M'Choakumchild (*Hard Times,* Charles Dickens)

So a person going into teaching could get their teaching credential, master's degree in education, and administrative credential in a span of three years. But let's give it four years as it's not always possible with time constraints and life as it happens. Let's also assume that they are teaching while concurrently taking the courses in order to get the teaching experience required to become an administrator.

This ultimately leads to a person who could be an administrator with just four years of classroom experience. And since the minimum number of years for many states (with few exceptions) is only two years of being a teacher, then we now have a Nouveau Administrator with only four years of experience in working with students. These are people who after only four years are barely getting the hang of using the student information system and posting grades, and yet they can become part of a school or even district administration.

Of course, the idea of keeping a single job for four years may be somewhat privileged, right? After all, with the market being what it is, layoffs and downsizing are all too real for any industry. But if you've been lucky enough to have what some call a "career" (whatever job you do for the majority of your life) for more than that, you know how little you know after that long, regardless of what the industry is, because at that point you're still figuring out the basics of how the basics work in terms of what you're doing and for whom. Eventually, you connect dots and meet enough people that you understand who has power over what. And while it's not kind to start implying Faustian overtones, you have to wonder how many are willing to abandon a ship that they feel others are just too lacking in the kind of research-based, achievement-gap-closing, rigor-increasing, socio-emotionally-adaptable, ESL-Inclusive, IEP-fulfilling, State-Board-Mandated-Compliance fulfilling, SBAC/PARCC-Score-improving, Graduation-Rate-Increasing almighty vision that they see so clearly enough as to decide to try and enter a bureaucratic position that involves as little interaction with students as possible. That's right, the people with the least interaction with the students are those that make the decisions—such as what classes a school should offer—for those same students... just sit and think about that one for a few minutes.

—

One thing you may not know if you aren't, or even if you are, in education is that it is possible for a teacher to become an administrator without the proper paperwork. If a teacher is good friends with the board and superintendent, then they can simply create a generic position called a Teacher On Special Assignment (TOSA). This workaround allows the board to give a teacher almost any title they want along with the pay and benefit perks if they so choose to include them. I know of teachers who were given principal and vice principal jobs without the proper paperwork, but because the board bequeathed them as TOSAs, they were then allowed to be an administrator without the paperwork needed to be an administrator. Although I've yet to hear of an assistant superintendent or even a superintendent position given through the title of TOSA, I wouldn't put it past them or be surprised if it has been attempted, and even succeeded.

Please understand that a TOSA is not always about the board trying to find some backdoor to get one of their lackeys into an administrative position who doesn't have the proper paperwork. A TOSA position is usually created when there is no specific title available for a particular teacher whose expertise could be used to help out the rest of the staff. But as with anything in education that is usually setup to help out the students, there will always be abuses by those in the position to abuse. I'd add something here about the 504 plan, but that would take a chapter unto itself; and if you're in education, you know exactly what I'm talking about.

Regardless as to whether those pieces of paper were assigned by the state or a local board of education trying to circumvent the rules, those in possession of them are the people who set the parameters by which a school district is run regardless of how little, if any, observation of the effect these people making the decisions are likely to have. And it is because of these pieces of paper that the people running the district are paid the six-figure salary that they so well deserve—I think the sarcasm alert just went off for that last sentence (where's Steven Wright when you need him?). They are the ones that make the decision to remove those pragmatic classes that teach about practice as opposed to just theory; those classes that I wrote about earlier that teach a real-life skill to students who are not interested in spending at least four more years and tens of thousands of dollars for something they may never use. They do this because they do not understand how those classes can teach a skill and help a student better understand something that they might be tested on: think drafting and geometry.

They are the ones suffering from a severe case of myopia when it comes to what they think has a positive impact on the school sites of which they are in charge. And regardless as to whether or not they are right or wrong when it comes to something for a school, they are always right.

A master's degree in education is almost as worthless when it comes to actual pragmatism as that of the majority of classes taken to earn a teaching credential. Nearly every person that I have spoken to about getting that master's degree in education has been very candid and also openly admitted that it was all about moving over a few columns in order to bump up their take-home pay; which will also increase how much they will be receiving in their retirement years.

Granted, that having a master's degree in education does allow for one to quote certain authors which, if you are in education, you have heard relentlessly in meetings somewhere at some time. It also does make for interesting discussions on pedagogical theory; but as we all know, theory and practice (at least when it comes to education) are often mutually exclusive.

Marge: *I really think this is a bad idea.*

Homer: *Marge, I agree with you, in theory. In theory, communism works, in theory.*

(The Simpsons)

Now, I know I wrote quite a bit about this in my previous book and it does sound repetitive (unless you didn't read it, in which case this might seem like not enough), but it really needs to be stressed as these are the people who decide what education "is" in this country. If you are in the field of education or just an observer who is quite thankful that you are not, hopefully you realize that there is no possibility that those in charge of many school districts—from the local school board to those that they put in place to run the district and the school sites—have the foresight to figure out what classes are needed to help students transition to a post-secondary life and whether or not college is part of that future... any better than the teacher who has known the student for oftentimes at least two years, if not their entire lives, depending on the district and the attrition rate. It's almost offensive to imagine we'd be able to determine a student's best interest without their input in the first place, but at the very least defer to the people who've had the most communication, right?

I can assure you that a master's degree in education, along with an administrative credential, does not give anyone who is in possession of these documents any sort of vision regarding what really is needed to help a student succeed once they graduate from high school. And yet, these people, along with the board of education, are the ones that have final say when it comes to what classes are being offered to students; not to mention the decision makers when it comes to how the money is spent.

The only way that they will ever figure out what types of classes could help to educate a student beyond that of standardized testing would be if: a) they accidentally come across an article or video on the internet somewhere that explains how some school, somewhere, in some other state took the initiative to start offering more variety of classes that were outside the core curriculum and somehow their scores went up, or b) they attend some conference somewhere in some other state (the cost of these thousand dollar plus trips will be paid for by the district) with the title: "*How To Implement A Paradigm Shifting Hands-on Curriculum In The 21st Century*," and how for the small sum of $50k, these people will come to your district and train all of the teachers in this new paradigm shifting, progressive teaching system that will change how both teachers and students view the educational process. And without even discussing with teachers in the district that have been there—in some instances for decades—for many years and have seen so many of these programs come and go, they will find a way to get funding to pay for it irrespective as to where the money is coming from.

I actually just made that last title for a program up off the top of my head, but I honestly wouldn't be surprised if it did indeed exist, and also to use it as a generic placeholder for anything that RAD comes across and just assumes that it will be as effective as the presenters made it sound (there should be an equation for the degree to which the creation of a zesty buzzword will increase the chances of an idea being purchased by a school district... let's call it the "Bureaucratic-Utterance-of-Linguistic-Liability-Signifying-Hierarchical-Intelligence-Theatre" [check the acronym on that one] factor). But this is pretty much how it all works. I know this because many schools in the area are having all of their teachers attend the latest fad in educational panacea which, for the moment, is Project Based Learning (though Design-Based Learning (DBL) is moving up the leader board). These PBL trainings are put on by specific companies that are making a fortune on the desperateness of so many school districts to increase their test scores.

Let me talk about PBL for just a moment, as there may be some confusion as to what my position is on the subject. Trying to cram multi-week grade-level projects into any class where the majority of students are already below grade level is simply an exercise in futility. Over the last couple of years the expectation is for teachers is to not only cover the curriculum that we already have trouble finishing in the allotted time frame, but to also insert some sort of project somewhere into that timeline, and catch those students up to grade level who can barely read, write, or do basic arithmetic beyond that of the 4th or 5th grade. Also take into account that RAD wants teachers to give more practice tests to better prepare students for the end of the year standardized testing, and you can see how this compounds to the degree where teaching really is becoming less of just that, and more about doing the things that those with the paperwork vision as the teaching and learning process.

So am I against project based learning? No! If you have made it this far then you realize what I'm trying to accomplish is to bring back a modern day version of those classes (along with getting rid of those useless administrative positions that will save districts hundreds of thousands of dollars) that we used to offer that are almost entirely comprised of projects—as well as teaching an actual skill—instead of trying to stuff it into an already full, and increasing curriculum. The teachers already have enough on their plates when it comes to teaching the topics that need to be covered from August to June. And in case you were wondering the answer is *no*, adding more days to the school year will not fix the existing problems as administration will find a way to waste those days as well.

The fact that administration is so willing to pay tens of thousands of dollars (that money could easily be used to help reduce the amount of fundraising students would have had to do for that specific year) for training teachers or attending conferences, and acting as if classroom projects have never happened before is asinine to say the least. All it goes to show is the ignorance of the people at the top pressing for this when they are the same people who are eliminating the project based classes that schools at one time used to offer. They speak of PBL as if it had never existed until these institutes that can come to a school district and train the teachers for whatever it is that they are charging came along and changed the paradigm... ugh.

By the way, congratulations to all of those companies that manage to get those despondent districts to pay you all of that money for something that used to be part of a standard curriculum. And don't worry, as long as RAD exists, you will be able to continue to get school districts that they work for to pay you whatever your fee is in order to help quell their appetite for pedagogical panacea.

—

With all of this talk of being progressive, the only thing that seems to be progressing is time. Schools continue to travel down the same path as they had the previous year, allowing the people that make the decision to get one step closer to retirement; they are fully aware that each year that passes takes them one step closer to those golden years. I am almost convinced that the reason many school district officials like to keep things status quo is because any sort of real change would require effort and work on their part, whereas keeping things the same and just paying lip-service to the surrounding community takes very little effort, if any at all. Administrators actually create more problems than they solve; which allows them to keep their position as the problems that they create are the next ones on the list that need to be solved, thereby justifying a need for their position.

This is how "education" for hundreds, if not thousands, of students at any one district is decided. It's a small group of people sitting at the district office dictating what they think is important for students to learn based on something that they read in some book during their master's degree classes, or when they were enrolled in an online class to get their administrative credential, or at one of many conferences that they will attend during the school year.

You know, RAD, if you really want to be progressive, why not change the six-period day (seven for some schools) into a five or even four-period day? Perhaps learning more about fewer subjects would be more beneficial than learning a little about more subjects. And the answer is yes—if the local board of education really wanted to make that type of schedule happen, they could manage it. I mean if they always manage to find money to hire a new administrator (or attend yet another all expenses paid, three-day conference) after telling teachers time and time again that the district is broke, then they can find the means to make this type of modification. With the whole *everyone-goes-to-college* movement (which won't be changing anytime soon) in full swing, why not change the school day to represent a college class schedule? All of this talk of being progressive (once again, the new *in* word that is used in lieu of, or in addition to, the ever popular phrase "paradigm shift"), and yet the class schedule for a student is the same as it was forty years ago with the exception that there are less classes available for a student to take.

As much as administration claims that they are being progressive, it doesn't really seem like they know what the meaning of the word really is. Block scheduling, minimum fifty percent grading policy (even if you didn't read my previous book you can already figure out my stance on that), and re-introducing what would be the equivalent of fourth and fifth-grade math classes at the high school level; these are just a few of the things that have been implemented over that last three years that RAD considers being progressive.

Those three items mentioned in the previous paragraph were all labeled as "progressive" by at least one administrator that I spoke to regarding each of them. Then again, since they are using the word as an adjective, as it also carries with it enough ambiguity that pretty much anything could be considered as progressive. It's a tricky word, because it doesn't technically count as comparative (it's not "progessiver"), but when you imagine applying it to something, you have to unconsciously assume that there's some aim toward "progress", which you just assume must have to be better because it's progressing from whatever came before it; but what "progress" actually means to any of the involved stakeholders, nobody has actually clarified to any degree much more specific than "Go Education™!" or "College™ for All!" By the way, if you are already tired of the word "progressive" after just a few paragraphs of usage, then I don't blame you. Now imagine hearing it over and over again at every meeting throughout the school year, and every time an administrator speaks about the changes that are coming to the school. Is it as overused as "paradigm shift"? Not yet, but give it time.

———

It seems as though the higher the rung on the administrative ladder that a person ascends, the more they forget about the reality of what happens in a classroom on a day-to-day basis. But although they forget about what really goes on in a classroom, what they think they know versus what they actually know seem to be converging on mutual exclusivity. In fact, if you take the torque graph from chapter five, all you need to do is change the vertical axis to how much RAD knows about teaching, and the horizontal axis to the number of years of being an administrator and, well you get the picture.

"It is difficult to get a man to understand something, when his salary depends on his not understanding it." – Upton Sinclair

So for those of you wondering why education seems to be going nowhere, then you need look no further than the current educational construct whereby the top-heavy, six-figure administration that not only take millions out of a districts annual budget, but are also the people that make the decisions that affect what is being taught in the classroom getting very little, if any, input from those that teach the classes (sycophantic teachers being the exception).

This is nothing new as it is the same educational model that has been in place for too many decades to count and it won't be changing, at least for the better, anytime soon. There are simply too many people dependent on the system as it stands in its current state. Understand once again, that when I talk about administration that I am speaking about our favorite revolving door administrator: RAD.

There is a long list of people who depend on the routine and torpidity of public education. Starting from the top, the quarter-of-a-million dollar superintendent whose monthly cell phone and car allowances (in many cases) add up to more than the monthly food budget for families in the district that they serve (or at least pretend to do so). This is especially evident if the top administrator works in a low-income, inner-city school district. The majority do whatever it is they need to (translated as doing what the board of education tells them to do) in order to keep their job; all the while looking for that next giant step to a bigger district that will offer them an even bigger car and cell phone allowance as well as a higher salary. And no matter how many jobs RAD has had, and no matter how many districts they bounce between, they will—with very few exceptions—always find another administrative job.

This also goes for the multiple assistant superintendents that are all vying for the top job once it becomes available at either their current district of employment, or whatever district is willing to hire them for the top position. They will carefully thread the line not to irk too many people (mainly the ones above them on the ladder) so as to not only keep their six-figure job, but remain on good terms with those that have their fate of a higher paying job in their hands. Each of the many will carefully step on each other's toes and throw the others under the bus when possible without drawing attention to their actions. Why is it that I just had a vision of Napoleon and Snowball?

Now drop one rung on the ladder and you are sitting in the principal's office. These are the people that are trying to keep their job just long enough to either get the promotion to district office administration, or to climb up a step at another school district. Much like the assistant superintendents, they won't make any drastic moves that might upset those above them, but will have no problem doing so with the teachers, counselors, and other support staff that are not in their trusted inner circle.

Under them are the multiple vice principals at the site who are barely getting their shoes wet when it comes to the daily ins-and-outs of being an administrator. Much like every single person in each position above them on the ladder, they will walk that fine line in order to stay on good terms with the people above them that will eventually decide when they finally get that promotion to a bigger office and higher paying job. It would be a rat-race, except that instead of destitution on the line, the rats have only the frustration of having to face the increased likelihood as one utterly incompetent of actualizing even a vague fraction of the kinds of change they are deluding themselves into implementing for yet another year; all the while trying to find a better-paying district. The struggle is ~~real~~... absolutely unknown to them.

Then there is the occasional sycophantic department chair that lets a little bit of power (which they don't have but they think they do) get to their head. These department chairs (not all, but if you are in education you know exactly about whom I am writing) don't realize that they don't have any authority over anyone, but because their sycophantic behavior is usually rewarded by RAD, then they will enjoy little perks such as the ability to handpick what classes that they want to teach; which never includes a remedial class. All the while the class schedule for rest of the teachers, for the most part, is simply a matter of happenstance. This, of course, is only able to be accomplished after the last chair retired who remembered the times when one would get an extra prep *and* a stipend for serving the duties, which included heavily influencing the master schedule each year. The reality is that this small subset of department chairs as well as RADs, really just represent the sidekick of a bully who will kick whoever is down once the bully has done the heavy lifting.

Let's not forget about the small handful of teachers with whom we have all worked with at one point or another; those who have their tenure and are high enough up on the seniority list such that they know they have a job as long as they want it. These are the ones who just sit back and press the play button knowing full well that they have a job (with the exception of those who commit some sort of heinous act that merits immediate removal from their position) until they decide to retire.

"And that's how it went for Andy—that was his routine. I do believe those first two years were the worst for him, and I also believe that if things had gone on that way, this place would have got the best of him." – Red (The Shawshank Redemption, 1994)

Let's also include all the other teachers that have become accustomed to the daily routine of education as well as a consistent paycheck, and the few times a year when we get to rest and recoup (although most of us just use the time dreading the return clinging to our metaphorical spoon—once again, extra credit if you know what book I'm referencing—but not just because of the students) after dealing with those enabled students and parents and, worse yet, the ultimate enabler of those just mentioned: RAD.

And how about those colleges that are getting more and more students applying each year as many high schools continue to lower the bar to keep those graduation rates up? Yes, they have to offer more remedial classes, but in the end, those classes are always full of unprepared college freshmens (only spelling it that way because I've worked with multiple principals who pronounced it that way, and not by accident, which does at least make one wonder what a plural of a plural would have to be...). These are the students that were pushed through by their respective high schools who end up paying for classes that do not even count toward a college degree; nor should they. And since many of these students end up taking these classes multiple times, the cash register is ringing for both the college and especially for those publishing the books.

Let's not leave the testing people off of this list. No, I'm not talking about the tests that the students take, as I have written plenty about that, but all of the testing needed to become a teacher and the companies that create, grade, and most importantly, charge up-and-coming teachers a nice chunk of change to take their exams. For those of you not in education, although you are probably mindful of the big business of standardized testing when it comes to students, you might not be aware of the big business of testing when it comes to getting a job in education (not to mention the state, at least California, getting a fee for a teacher credential renewal every five years).

There's even a certain (intentionally) unnamed entity that has taken upon itself to trademark the term "Accomplished Teacher™," which is something that anyone would do well to question as to the degree to which they are measuring that which needs to be accomplished.

Let's also not forget the book publishers that are rapidly trying to figure out how they are going to continue to make money when they will no longer be able to sell physical copies of books to schools at one hundred plus dollars apiece once people go to all digital. Then again, this isn't really a difficult solution for them to figure out. Most K–12 schools go through an adoption period once every x years (x = 7 for my school; well at least it's supposed to be seven. But as you saw from the picture of the social science books, this isn't always the case). So the digital books will most likely be more of a profit maker as they will probably charge by the year and always make sure to have an update or two that represents just enough of a change from the previous version for schools to pay up for the next installment. As far as social science is concerned, this is probably a pretty good idea. But as for math and some sciences, if administration ever realized that an HBJ algebra book used in the '80s are just as good as the algebra books for today that they could get for a tenth, if not less, of the cost, then some of these book publishers might be in trouble. But then again, we are dealing with RAD, so I don't think the publishers need to worry about this happening... ever.

Of course you might be thinking as to why anyone would want to use a book from the '80s instead of the newer books with all the amazing graphics. Well for one thing, the HBJ algebra book is one of the best that I've ever worked out of and still have a set that I keep in my classroom (I kept as many I could that were in decent shape before the rest were thrown out when I first started teaching). And as far as the graphics are concerned (as they are definitely out of date), if you really want some nice pictures to demonstrate for the class, just use your favorite search engine and find whatever images that are needed for the lesson. But if you look at an algebra book today in comparison to one from back then (not taking into account the pretty pictures from today's books and the outdated word problems from the books of yesteryear), you really won't find much difference in regards to content. The one thing that you might notice is that today's versions don't have as much because publishers are meeting the needs of the schools that are all watering down their curriculum, and focused more on topics of standardized testing as opposed to learning something for the sake of just that.

—

With so many people making so much (or little depending on the position) money off of the educational system as it currently stands, then why would they be in any rush to change that which is the basis for their livelihood?

Then there are the people that depend on the system but for different reasons. There are the parents of students who depend on the free meals that their kids get when they go to school each and every day. Many families in an inner-city school district have less money to spend on food than a superintendent receives for their monthly car allowance. Of course, don't expect any superintendent to give up that car allowance anytime soon.

Now I can keep going as there are a lot of gaps that I missed when it comes to much of the support staff such as food services, school security, and the custodial staff. But the point is that there are a very many people who depend on the system to stay in its current state. They have become acclimated to the daily, monthly, and annual routine of public education.

And this is the main reason that education is such a slow moving, bureaucratic shamble. Most school districts will never improve fast enough to keep up with what students should know to survive in the real world, as the people making the decisions do not realize that going slower than the outside world is detrimental to the people that they have been hired to help and prepare to succeed in the outside world.

Administration is the *rate determining step* of a school district. If you paid attention in chemistry, a rate determining step is the slowest step of a chemical reaction that dictates how fast the rest of the reaction occurs. In other words, the rest of the reaction cannot go faster than its slowest step, and this is exactly how a school district works.

To put this in terms of going around in circles, which is sort of a point of expertise for school districts, the auto-racing term would be the "pace car", which while in racing limits the speed of competing racers, in education only enables those with the proper paperwork to set the pace of what they believe should be learned. No matter how many assessments are claiming to address the upper Depth of Knowledge (DOK) levels, or Bloom's Taxonomy (to which they are always bound, aren't they?), we know that there is a level of consciousness that is required in order to process a certain level of thought. So unless we want to grant rights to the AI bots reading student essays on turnitin.com, we need to very quickly decide where we draw the line on our dependence on technology as there are already bots writing articles, at least for many of the major media outlets (https://www.nytimes.com/interactive/2015/03/08/opinion/ sunday/algorithm-human-quiz.html).

What's important to understand is that moving slowly doesn't actually matter to administration no matter how many times they say it does. They will continue to make their promises about one thing or another, but also talk about how these steps that they just presented take time to implement. They will do and say what they need to in order to keep their high paying job not realizing that their inability to adjust is affecting the students who they claim that they are putting first.

"Listen, I'm a politician; which means I'm a cheat and a liar. And when I'm not kissing babies, I'm stealing their lollipops." – Jeffery Pelt (The Hunt For Red October, 1990)

———

Whether you like it or not, the system is going to stay as it is unless something comes along that causes such a shock that school districts are forced to change the way they do business. The main problem is that the people who would be in charge of changing the district would be those very same six-figure administrators who are already making the decisions that affect everyone below them from teachers to students. The only difference this time around is that the administrators would more than likely give themselves a raise before figuring out another short-term solution to the problems that ail.

It's easy for someone reading this to think that I am anti-administration. This is partly true as I am definitely anti RAD, who represents an extremely large subset of the entire set of school administration for most school districts across the country. The problem is that RAD is rapidly becoming the rule as opposed to exception (they may already be the rule). With the simplicity as it is for a person to get the degrees and credentials to become an administrator, and with very little when it comes to actual pre-requisites to becoming an administrator, RAD is simply going to be part of the educational construct until something gives to the point where people realize that the decisions made by RAD represent the beginning of the majority of the problems that schools have when it comes to the inner workings of a school system.

If there was one thing that could help at least some of the problems with the system as it currently stands, it's that there should be restrictions as to what educational experience a person needs in order to become an administrator at a particular school. Similarly as I wrote in my last book, a teacher that has only elementary school experience should not be allowed (at least immediately) to be an administrator of a high school and vice-versa.

———

A colleague a few doors down (a very level-headed individual, and probably one of the nicest people I've ever met) who has been with this district for his entire teaching career and will be retiring in another three years or so, admitted that he has never seen the district in the shape as it currently stands. He has seen entire administrations come and go; a superintendent having her teaching and administrative credential suspended; a principal who would sit in the back of his classroom to make him as uncomfortable as possible in order to get him to transfer (which worked), and survived a school board whose Gestapo-like tactics eventually lead to a colleague committing suicide. And yet, after all of this and much more, he admits that he has never seen this district in as much disarray as it is in its current state.

For this specific school year (2017–2018), two of the administrators (one of which walks in at least twenty minutes late almost daily and is being transferred to her fourth site in five years) are barely visible—with exception to meetings or a walkthrough when some important visitor to the school wants to visit classrooms and needs to be escorted from one classroom to the next that administration will select. The third administrator is doing what she can, but is having a difficult time to say the least, and does not seem to fully grasp that these are high school students and not elementary school students.

Students—usually the same ones on a daily basis—will walk around the school all period knowing that it is very unlikely that anyone (with exception to certain teachers and a small handful of campus monitors) will call them out on it. It's now at that point where teachers won't say anything to these students as they will usually talk back in a very undiplomatic fashion; and it really is not worth getting into an argument with a student that you as a teacher are not familiar with. I've been witness to these students walking right by the open door of the principal's office, buy something from the vending machine right outside, and just hang out there until they get bored and decide to move along, with the principal saying absolutely nothing to them as they wander around during class time.

Essentially, our school has been administrator-less for a number of years now. The superintendent, along with at least three other top people over at the district office, are currently interims; although it is very likely that the board will remove the *Interim* part of the title over the summer at a June or July board meeting as well as giving these people (who couldn't name ten students in the entire district) a nice raise to go along with it. The fate of the previous superintendent is given at the end of Coach's Story just in case you were wondering. And yes, it cost the district well over $200k to buyout the one year left on his contract. Our current principal and one vice principal are pretty much just ghosts hiding in their offices until the end of the year. The sum total of dollars for two people that do very little is costing the district (salary and benefits) well over $300k.

The main reason that the school is holding together as well as it has is because of the number of teachers who have been through this before and know how to handle what goes on in their own classroom. Most of the teachers on this campus all started around the year 2000 and have many years of experience when it comes to lack of support from administration. We are also quite cognizant that schools like this one (they are plenty in number) are used by many an up-and-coming RAD in order to climb a rung of the administrative ladder in the hopes of getting that higher paying job at whatever district will hire them—and yes, they will be hired.

Another reason that the school is holding together is because of the often overlooked and almost conspiratorially ignored support staff. Those include everyone from food services, campus monitors, custodial staff, the amazing secretaries, and everyone in between who are always the first to be let go when the budget is cut, or money is needed to hire another six-figure administrator. But without the support staff, the school would simply not be able to function. Don't think for a second that RAD has any idea how hard these people work to keep the school running as seamlessly as possible and how little they are appreciated. For those of you who think teaching is a thankless job, try being one of the support staff.

The secretary of the curriculum office is doing more to help problematic students get to class than two of the three administrators on campus. She is finding and escorting those particular students that are trying to find a place to ditch and walking them to their classes which—I know with one hundred percent certainty—is not anywhere in her job description. And by the way, if you are a Neophyte in education and are not really sure how the system works, take this pro tip and be *very* nice to all of the support staff, but especially to the secretaries and custodians on campus. They will help you more with the daily ins-and-outs of being at work than any RAD extant (or future ones for that matter). It's also important to keep in mind that they will be around long after the current RAD, the next one, and the one after that, have moved on to shift the paradigm at other sites either within the same district, or some other district somewhere that decided to give them a job.

—

Testing actually went fairly smooth this year; but it was only because of the secretary (the same person mentioned in the previous paragraph) in the curriculum office was running the show. She put the rosters together for the teachers, assigned teachers and students to computer labs, and showed up early to school in order to deliver snacks (with the help of the custodians) to the multiple computer labs where the testing was taking place. In other words, she did all of the work that the curriculum vice principal was supposed to be doing, but for nowhere near the pay of an administrator. These are educators who require no certificate to prove their commitment.

"Badges? We don't need no stinking badges." – Rick Garcia (Blazing Saddles, 1974)

There are plenty of other schools out there in a similar state of disorder that may not have as many veteran teachers with the experience that we currently have, which is why we have been able to, at least for the time being, hold things together. I'm sure there are other revolving door school districts out there that also have teachers moving in and out about as often as their administration. And if you happen to work at a school with both high administration and teacher turnover and are somehow surviving, and still managing to make a difference in the lives of those who pass through your classroom while taking on the number of battlefronts with those enabled students and parents, administration, as well as other teachers, then you definitely deserve to be paid more than those administrators who sit back in their chair and delegate their responsibilities to others; hopefully one day this will happen.

So where does it all go from here? Well, in short, nowhere. Things will stay the same even though administration will continue to tell the public that major changes are being made thanks to all of the amazing new technology that is being purchased through some bond issuance. But the reality is that all of the purchases being made and displayed are just a facade in the hopes of distracting the public from what really happens within the confines of a school district.

If you have been in the system long enough, you come to the realization that the solutions that are presented by the current administration are pretty much the same as the previous administration, which are the same as those who came before, and so on.

"A poet once wrote: meet the new boss, same as the old boss." – Dressler (The Sum of All Fears, 2002 (and of course, The Who – Won't Get Fooled Again, 1971))

If you have been at a school like the one I work at long enough, you know there is plenty of potential for the school to transcend its own stereotype. But this will never happen and the problems will only to continue to worsen as long as school district administration continue to depend on a magical pedagogical miracle acronym (MPMA) that will present itself at one of the many conferences that they will attend throughout the year. Instead of trying to work out a solution, they are simply taking the same path that so many students do by searching for something to tell them what the solution is that will solve their problems. And just like many students, they are working harder at trying to find a ready-made generic solution as opposed to taking the necessary steps to figure out a unique solution—as each school is unique, especially when it comes to its own set of issues—to the problems that the schools in the district are facing.

Although I'm sure someone out there is putting a new acronym together to sell to despondent districts promising that their strategy will definitely work because they have their own unbiased data that shows its efficacy. And of course, after an hour long presentation at some three-day conference, there will be plenty of administrators ready to pay up whatever the asking price might be because this time, under their administrative leadership, is definitely going to be different.

I hate to break it to those of you trying to find that magic elixir that will fix everything for a one-time substantial fee, but if it hasn't been discovered by now, then it's probably not going to be found at a presentation right before lunch at one of your many three-day conferences.

Is it possible that the next remedy that administration spends tens of thousands of dollars on after only watching a short presentation and a couple of "unbiased" YouTube videos will work? Yes, it could. But it can't possible make things worse than they were before, right? Well, if you've been in education long enough, you know that not only can it be worse, but at some point, it probably will be.

Bart: *This is the worst day of my life.*

Homer: *The worst day of your life so far.*

(The Simpsons Movie, 2007)

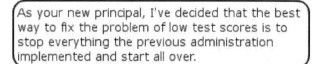

As your new principal, I've decided that the best way to fix the problem of low test scores is to stop everything the previous administration implemented and start all over.

Instead of wasting time and money starting over, why not ask the teachers what has worked in the past and build upon that?

Because you don't have an administrative credential and don't understand what proactive pedagogical strategies work best in your classroom.

- 13 -

Technology Faux Pas

I recently found out I was a "Xennial." This means that since I was born between the six-year span of 1977-1983 (in the first of those years, actually), I belong to a special "micro-generation" that forms a bridge between the Millennials and the Gen-Xers; at least according to people who have the proper connections to legitimize this sociological theory and spread it to people like me. To tell the truth, I don't really hold a lot of stock in treating generations like monolithic cultures.

But it did get me thinking.

My first classroom teaching experience was a substitute job at a high school built in the 1930s as a WPA project (part of Roosevelt's "New Deal" that would later be credited with helping to end the Great Depression (or prolong it, depending on your economic bias)). It was 2004, so I'd have been 27 at the time.

The walls were solid brick, and there were perhaps 4 outlets in the 60' x 45' space (if I'm retrospectively eyeballing it). There was a teacher's desk, a chalkboard (yes, an actual chalkboard; it was at the tail end of what I call the "whiteboard-washing" of the American classroom (tongue-in-cheek, of course)), and an AV-cart which included a 30" cathode ray tube television (the big ones with rabbit-ears, if you'd forgotten that they exist... as I occasionally do, I must admit) and a VCR and—get this—a Laserdisc player (you might have to google this, even if you are old enough to remember as they were not exactly the most popular of playback devices).

But there was a computer on the teacher's desk, and that computer had internet access. There was also another device in the room, which the regular teacher admitted he had no idea how to operate in the slightest, and he said he just let them install it there because it would impress RAD. It was called a "Smart Board", and I later found out it cost $10,000.

He taught English, I think. His lesson plans for the three-day absence included exclusively and entirely the instructions to play videos of *The Twilight Zone* and have students write responses to the episodes. He left a list of episodes he recommended, but said that I should feel free to play one of my favorites for them if it was included in the box-set.

I then took the opportunity to run copies of an article from the 1899 conflict in the Philippines and compare it to an article about the then-current "war" (technically a "military action", like a certain other previous war... and the one before that) in Iraq. Suffice it to say that it didn't go over well, but that's a different story. The point here is that technology in the classroom (or at all, really) is only as useful as the degree to which it is used, regardless of the purpose toward which it is directed.

One of the defining factors of us Xennials (and let's face it, there are plenty of those born earlier who managed to stay a bit younger at heart to be grandfathered (in some cases literally) into the group—let's not be ageist here...) is that we were alive and coming into our own during a time which saw the personal computer do what television did in the '50s—become the primary medium of distribution of information among the middle-to-upper-middle class.

I played Oregon Trail in third grade on an Apple IIE, and when my dad got our family an Apple IIGS a few years later, after borrowing a slightly older model from his school over the summer (he was also a teacher—English, even), I fell in love.

Flash forward 30 years, and I find it difficult to believe that there is still resistance to teaching digital literacy in the classroom by using and working with computers (the ones with keyboards) and understanding the structure of how they work—the OS (Operating System) type. The idea of programs (well, I guess they're called "Apps" now basically, but there used to be a difference—it's short for "Application", and it used to just run a function of a program instead of being an entirely separate thing) and browsers and the functionality of each, and word processors and spreadsheets, and basically all of the tools that have formed the entirety of the foundation of the business and professional world for the past three decades... but there is still some resistance—there really is.

I didn't get a classroom with more than one computer until my second year of full-time teaching, and it was a small cart of MacBooks—20, I think. Their batteries lasted about an hour and a half unplugged, and the security was locked down so tight that you couldn't use a flash-drive with the USB ports because IT was afraid they'd get viruses (yet the PCs were like the Times Square of flash-drives... I know some of you will appreciate the irony of this). They came equipped with Microsoft Office (for Mac, of course, because why use the native software when you can buy more for twice the price?), an internet browser (it may have been Internet Explorer, actually, because I don't even remember if they had Safari at the time or, if they did, whether or not it was usable), some various bloatware, and miscellaneous publisher apps for whatever textbook adoption was trying to prove it was "keeping up with the times" by offering some outsourced digital content. This either mirrored the textbook or linked to websites that always seemed to be either under construction or 404ed ("site not found"). The textbook market is a whole other story, though, and deserves its own book (of which many already exist—I recommend <u>Lies My Teacher Told Me</u> by James W. Loewen for a well-written and fantastic deconstruction).

Thanks to the restrictions of permissions for users due to security limitations within the native OS, and the inability to truly network the machines, this $30,000 cart of technology was about as useful as a pile of paperweights—because without a way to save any files to removable media, and no installable drivers for the classroom printer, there wasn't any way to transfer documents from device to device—it was a closed system with no way to communicate outside itself. I wound up leaving the laptops in a portable to which I was exiled while my classroom was being renovated (it was an asbestos abatement), and during which time I acquired a yearbook program and rightfully figured the cart would be better served as a camera checkout station, considering it was the only lockable cabinet to which I had access.

The other thing to which I didn't have much access when I took over the yearbook program was computers.

Previous to my brief tenure as yearbook advisor, there was a bit of a kerfuffle when the IT guy accidently forgot to include the external drive on which the entire yearbook was stored as accessible by the network. So he—being the previous yearbook teacher—thought he had lost everything, and by the time they had worked it out, the yearbook staff had already recreated a number of pages they'd already done, and the submission deadline had long since passed.

So in order to avoid this type of issue again, I decided (once I took over the yearbook class) to go to the cloud. The publisher had wisely made available a Java-based remediation of what was basically In Design (™ Adobe), but watered down enough so that it didn't require any external storage, and was entirely accessible from anywhere you had internet access. If you were born today (or probably within the past 5 years, really), consider yourself blessed for not considering that anything but a basic expectation.

The problem was that between all of the available "spare" computers from nearby classrooms (when you have four desktop computers for 35–40 students, you realize quickly that they're basically useless), I could only amass about 15 of them, which I built into a little self-contained computer lab with the assistance of extension cords, switches, and routers, even though the entire thing was coming out of a single ethernet drop (the IT guy later told me that my configuration "shouldn't have worked," and that he didn't understand why it did... but then again, he also missed a giant 1-TB external drive hanging from the center of the meager bevy of desktops which housed the entire yearbook, so it's safe to assume he lacked some vision).

I kept it going, despite the constant peril of Java updates requiring an admin password that might delay the project by anywhere from 2–3 days, depending on how many tech requests were before ours in the chain of various needs ranging from "my printer won't work," to "I deleted the System32 folder" (again, not many will appreciate that joke, but it's worth it to those who do). And let's also not forget those who would drag a program's desktop shortcut onto a 3.5" floppy disk and take it home thinking that they had brought with them the entire program. I actually had an administrator demonstrate this to me. He was honestly confused as to why the program wouldn't work on his computer at home... seriously!

The IT shortage in education is so severe that we don't even recognize it, because we don't realize the potential we have as it's been in effect for so long. I'm pretty sure 99% of schools haven't even seen what their full potential looks like. It wasn't until I was transferred to another school that I was finally able to go wireless.

———

I had lucked into another chance to take over another yearbook program, and this time it came with a choice (because the prior advisor had wisely gone to the cloud with their publisher, so I was just continuing a well-known process): I could either have a cart with 10 MacBooks, or a cart with 40 HP Streams (which were about equivalent to a Chromebook in terms of processing capacity, but with Windows 10 preinstalled instead of the ersatz-Linux Chrome OS).

There was no choice at all. We had just received Google accounts district-wide, including the students, so Google Classroom finally became a possibility to use, now that I had the necessary amount of resources to provide an actual 1:1 laptop-to-student ratio. Because of this, I may be the first person in my district to have a truly paperless classroom. And as good as that may sound, it was, in many ways, a complete nightmare.

A funny thing happens when you attempt to accomplish every task in an ELA classroom in a shared digital space: you uncover the depths to which digital literacy skills are lacking among the students. They pressed "Caps Lock" every time they needed to use a capital letter, which was essentially only when I reminded them that it was customary to capitalize their name, city, or any proper noun; which one would think that a high school student would already know.

As was mentioned in the chapter *The 21st Century Classroom*, just because students grow up only knowing a life with all of this technology, doesn't necessarily imply that they are as technologically advanced as RAD seems to believe. In fact, since most technology does our work for us, many students—as the years progress—seem to know less and less about how any of it really works.

———

I learned to type on an electric typewriter. My parents gave me a mechanical one for my 14th birthday (probably because they couldn't afford the Brother Word Processor—with 3.5" floppy drive for document storage—I wanted, but they tried to make do), and it wound up teaching me a lot; like why it's called a "Shift" button. But then I was texting and realized that when you hit "Shift" on a touch-screen keyboard, it toggles just like the Caps Lock button does, and the majority of students today literally don't see the difference.

"Punch the keys for god's sake." – William Forrester (Finding Forrester, 2000)

And this is the new, somewhat-hidden digital divide. Those who learned to type by touching a virtual keyboard (which means they have basically developed their own system of typing, because there's no systematized process for "learning to type" this way), and those of us who punched the keys.

However, there is a unifying structure between these two disparate frameworks, and it's the basic digital literacy skills that, once we can pin down and include it into the rest of the literacy-based curriculum of English/Language Arts, will bridge that divide. Trust me: I'm a Xennial.

But first, we have to get past the larger issue of figuring out how to distribute technology funds. They're usually earmarked, which means that if you don't spend the entire amount, then your future budget will be reduced to the amount that you spent the year prior, not to mention that they are supposed to be spent for that which they were received, and not shuffled around to be spent on something else... which means absolutely nothing to those with access as to how the funds are spent. Although this might sound reasonable, it's just another example of how theory and practice don't totally coincide with one another.

On my school site, there are approximately 200 Apple TVs (just in case you are not familiar with these, they are not actually televisions, but little black boxes used to play media similar to that of Roku). Literally, none of them were ever used in the classroom, or anywhere for that matter. Why? Well, as it turns out, in order to use an Apple TV, the user would first have to sync it up with another Apple device—which we had none of—and connect them to some monitor in order to view the content—which we also did not have. Apple is somewhat known for creating proprietary technology (dongles anyone?). But didn't they first check to make sure that their technology purchase would be something that could be used by every site? No. But more strikingly was the cost of these devices. The retail cost of the first generation of Apple TVs was $299 (let's round that to $300) which would bring the total to $60,000 plus tax and shipping. Now, it is possible that whoever made this purchase did a little shopping around and managed to eke out a small discount. But it's more than likely that any discount would have been just enough to cover the tax and shipping which would still yield a total of $60k.

It's that simple. The purchasing of technology is so decentralized (especially in a large district like mine), that there are often purchases made in haste that neglect to cross-reference the preexistent resources, and oftentimes by people who have no idea what they're purchasing (because the IT folk are in a different union than those who control the budget), that we wind up with exactly the kind of hodgepodge of various random outdated technology that decorates the creepy bat-cave you'll find on every campus. These are pretty easy to find if you look hard enough and know who to ask.

That's how we wind up with $10k Smart Boards in classrooms where nobody knows how to use them, or a cart of MacBooks that are but worthless when it comes to helping students with their assignments. So until we address the underlying issue and replace the Smart Boards of yesteryear with actual smart boards (of education), and take special care to ensure that the technology we're buying and distributing is being used in a way that promotes student learning, we're going to keep restocking the same overburdened supply rooms, resupplying the same earmarked budgets, and recreating the same problems.

Or we could just hope that the next generation will solve it. That seems to have worked pretty well so far, right? And just in case you weren't keeping track, the one Smart Board, the computer cart of Macs, and the 200 Apple TVs, gives us a grand total of about $100,000 for items that are no more than expensive dust collectors. Earmarked or not (which really doesn't mean anything as districts find ways to shuffle funds around all the time), think about what all of that money could have gone towards.

- 14 -

Coach's Story

Coach started teaching at a local inner-city high school in the early 2000s. His assignments would vary every year as his background and credentials allowed for him to teach a number of different subjects ranging from PE (which represents the majority of his teaching assignments), to typing, math, or economics. Regardless of his schedule, he was not averse to taking up a coaching assignment which, for his first five years, was varsity baseball; as well as heading the entire baseball program.

Coaching baseball was a pretty normal step for Coach, as he had many years of experience as well as playing college ball for a Division 1 school. He still has the baseball that he hit off Randy Johnson for a double back in his college days. In other words, he was a pretty good ball player in his time.

Coach took over the baseball program which—to say it nicely—needed a bit of an overhaul, as it had very little success for many of the previous years. He was, however, able to rebuild the program from the ground up and was also able to eke out a winning season his first year and only improved upon this result for the next four years.

The program itself was also building up from the freshman level which helped for future teams down the road. Coach also made sure that his players were accountable for what transpired in the classroom with respect to their grades as well as their behavior. He would talk to teachers individually if a student wasn't living up to the expectations of the classroom, and would tell the staff at meetings that the players were students first and athletes second. He also asked teachers to bring any issues to him directly in order to resolve the problems that they might be having with any of his players. And if those problems were to continue to cause issues in the classroom, the student would be benched—no questions asked—regardless of whether said student was or was not a starter.

But as per any job, there will always be disputes with people at a job site. In this case, the only troubles that Coach had for his first three years were with the varsity basketball coach. In short, the basketball coach did not want his players on the baseball team, mandating to his players that it was one sport or the other—but not both. Needless to say, this caused a little dissension between the two, but not something that was detrimental to the basketball or baseball programs... well, at least not in the beginning.

The first real conflict came when the same basketball coach took that giant leap into administration (and yes, most definitely a RAD from day one (he was also one of those teachers that would sit back in a chair and watch ESPN while his students did whatever)) during his third year as head coach. Suddenly, Coach is being called into the Nouveau Administrator's office and literally being told how to run a baseball program; from fund raising to the actual aspects of coaching a team, from someone that had zero days of baseball-coaching experience. It was quite obvious that Coach had a target on his back from what had occurred between the two when RAD was head of the basketball program.

Although this was definitely a hurdle—not to mention a continual burden for Coach to have to deal with—it wasn't enough to get him to quit. After all, he did put lots of time into the program for the last three years and was getting the results with winning records, playoff bids and, most importantly, players that understood that their role as an athlete came secondary to that of their education.

The real problems began when the new principal (which would have been his third principal in five years as well as his fifth season of coaching) from the world of vocational education took over the high school. Why the board and superintendent decided to go with a principal who had no teaching or administrative experience with a K–12 school is beyond me; but that's what we ended up with... for about fourteen months. The official reasoning was that she was brought in to make the cuts in the budget where the cuts were "needed" in order to save the district some money, which most of you know is a very bad call—but if you are in education, you kind of get used to the district office making those kinds of bad decisions.

The first thing that the new principal (whose strings were being pulled by the vice principal, which is a whole story unto itself, but not especially salient to this one) did was to get rid of sixth-period athletics, which was equivalent to a PE class but specifically for athletes. Since many of the students that play sports have to leave early for an event, having this class at the end of the day made sense as it would minimize students missing any of their curricula and allow them to work with their coaches for whatever sport they were involved with.

This was just another hurdle for Coach, along with the

coaches of other sports, to jump over. Of course, this move, when compounded with a new administrator micromanaging (as almost every administrator does) his every motion, really began to take its toll on him—and yet, he still did not give up.

Now, for those of you who are not directly involved in education, then it might seem as if these minutia-like moves would not be overly adverse for a coach and their team. But anyone who has ever had a job, any job, probably knows what it is like when a supervisor (or in this case multiple supervisors) makes decisions without consulting you and scrutinize every move you make under a microscope... then you probably know how Coach was starting to feel at this moment.

It was getting to the point when he really started to second guess whether he should continue to do what he was doing. After all, if you have ever coached a team or have been in charge of anything extracurricular, you know the hours after school can be long, and you certainly know the financial compensation is (as I wrote about earlier) about what minimum wage was back late '90s or early '00s. He also had to take into consideration that he had three kids of his own growing up and playing on their own teams, and that he would be (as he was already) missing their games, along with other events, to attend to his coaching duties.

The first thing the new principal asked of Coach was to tell the players (on both sides) not to hit the ball over the left-field fence. To better understand this, you need to be able to picture a baseball field with the left-field fence running parallel to the street in front of the school (a fairly common sight). The fence is surely higher than a normal fence, but some players do have the firepower to occasionally knock one over. But in the sixty years that the school has been around, a ball getting hit over the fence has never been an issue, so it's not a huge leap of logic to infer that the cause of this edict was something perhaps more personal.

Ironically, just as it was approaching that breaking point where Coach started to feel like his investment in the program was going underwater, the final straw was literally over water. As you may know, a baseball field is ideally a well-groomed space with green grass on the infield and outfield, along with that diamond shape of dirt along the baselines as well as that which makes the pitcher's mound. Well, they got the dirt part down pat, but neglected to recognize that in order for the grass to grow, hydration is required. The field was simply not getting enough water, and while the temptation to chalk it up to the California drought is there, it was not the case at that time, nor did the landscaping for other fields suffer in a similar fashion. The principal simply did not want to turn the water on for the baseball field.

Coach then decided to ask for the key so that he could set the timers for the sprinklers to go on at night. And why not ask for it? The football field was getting the water it needed (this was a few years before the artificial field was put in), the grassy areas in the school were on timers and had no problem staying green along with that of the trees, and that one patch of grass all the way at the end of the field behind the football scoreboard where no one ever traverses was also getting plenty of water, but not the baseball field. When coach asked for the key the response was a simple *no*. He then asked if one of the custodians could set the timer instead; the answer was still *no*.

This was that moment that Coach simply said enough is enough. No support from administration, missing out on his kids playing baseball and softball, a former basketball coach turned administrator breathing down his neck for everything he does and finally, no water. So Coach finished out his fifth and final winning season and decided to never take on another coaching position for the school again. And if you haven't already figured out his personality, "never" was about six years away.

About five years and two principals (not including a couple of interims) later (I couldn't even tell you how many vice principals), Coach was approached and asked if he would be willing to take over the football program for the next school year. Understand that the football program at this school was... well, there really wasn't much of one at the time. The school had not had a winning season in many years and was also a revolving door for coaches in the same manner as it was, and still is, for administrators.

Let me take a step back for a moment. The principal and vice principal of the old regime were gone. They were removed right before winter break during the next school year (after Coach had resigned) and given some job over at the district office until the end of the school year which they were then dismissed. The vocational principal experiment was over.

One of the first things that the new principal did once she took over midway through the year was to ask Coach if he would be willing to take the baseball position back. This principal had known him for many years and knew that he was not only a good coach, but also good for the kids. And although he did think about and consider it, he felt that taking a hiatus from any after school activities was the best thing for him and, more importantly, his kids.

Now back to taking over what was a number of consecutive losing seasons for the football program at this particular high school. The school's team would win one or two games per year including pre-season (there was at least one year of zero wins). The new principal wanted to change that and try to bring some winning spirit back to the school.

By now Coach's eldest and middle were both away attending college and the youngest was in high school. So if he wanted to get back into that of his namesake, then now would probably be as good a time as any.

He went into his first meeting with some skepticism but found that, at least face-to-face, the new principal really wanted to work with him. The meeting came down to Coach listing what it was he would need in order to run the best program possible. He then told the principal that if he was given what was on the list that he would take the job.

After submitting the list, his first thought was that they [being the new administration] would never approve it, or would pretend they approved and renege on it afterward (happens much more than you might think). A few days passed and coach was finally called into the principal's office to discuss the list of demands. Surprisingly, everything on the list was approved.

"Peculiar thing about this document; it was never notarized." – Lucy Van Pelt (It's The Great Pumpkin, Charlie Brown, 1966)

Coach started immediately.

The next day there was an announcement over the PA system that any students interested in playing football for Coach next year should attend a meeting later that week. The meeting was packed.

——

For the last few years, the football team would be lucky to get twenty students to play on the team. And of those twenty, many would not show up to practices because the previous coaches simply did not have the high standards of accountability that Coach brings to the field. Many of the returning players were told to shape up and to show up to practices, or they would not be allowed to play on the team.

The end result was that Coach lost a lot of the would-be returners and had a team made up mostly of sophomores with little playing experience. This, however, did not deter him from building up the program. He knew that the first year with new players would not be an easy one and did not have high expectations because of the lack of experience. And even though the first season was a tough one, they were still able to win three games that year; this might not sound like much, but the previous coaches won three games in the last three years combined, and that was with one season of zero wins. So this was quite an accomplishment for a new coach with a younger, inexperienced squad.

The next three seasons were all improvements upon that of the first and came with the school's first post-season CIF appearance (during year two) in eight years. Things were finally looking good for the football program and Coach was getting recognition from the local newspaper for what he accomplished in such a short amount of time.

Then came yet another new administration (you probably already know where this is going). A new superintendent was brought in by the new board majority and, along with a new superintendent, comes new site administration regardless of how qualified they are or, in many cases (especially this case), are not for the positions that they are given... that's right, given. Yes, there were shams of interviews but in the end, many of the principal and vice principal positions in the district went to the friends of the new superintendent (don't act so surprised).

For some reason the new vice principal in charge of discipline (of which he did very little when it came to discipline) was not very fond of Coach and, in a similar fashion to that of the basketball coach turned administrator, this person simply wanted to tell Coach how to run the program, and acted as if he was the one in charge; even though his job description had nothing to do with coaching nor being in charge of anything that had to do with athletics. But since this person and the new superintendent were friends from way back, whatever this particular RAD would tell the superintendent is what the superintendent would believe with respect to what went on over at the high school. In case you didn't read my previous book *The Need For Common Core*, or even if you did, here is a reminder of that person.

This RAD just felt like he should be the one in charge of the football program and, at least from the perspective of those familiar with the situation, it also appeared as if he wanted the coaching job for himself.

What also began to happen was that suddenly Coach found himself in a position where the support from administration was beginning to fizzle out... again. They also began to ignore items that were promised to him from the previous administration in regards to the list that was approved in the agreement for him to take the job.

The biggest item on the list was that the football program would get half of the gate and snack-bar money in order to support the needs for the team along with giving stipends to the assistant coaches (whom the district was not willing to pay). This might sound like a lot of money but being that, at least for the first season, there would be maybe one hundred people on average in the stands, at best half of the gate would be around three-hundred dollars. And since only half of the season were home games, multiply that three-hundred by four (this also included pre-season games) and you get a whopping twelve-hundred (plus a few hundred more from the concessions) dollars to add to a meager budget that the new administration was already cutting—along with all other activity budgets.

The good news though, was that each subsequent season brought with it a higher number in the wins column which helped to increase the attendance for the home games. It actually got to the point that by the fourth season, the home side would be filled from end-to-end. Considering that the very first game during that first season had (and this is being generous) about—if you include the band—a total of maybe of sixty people in attendance, filling up the stands was quite an accomplishment.

This takes us to the night of the homecoming game of Coach's fourth year of running the football program. By the estimates, there were probably about twenty-five hundred people in attendance for the entire stadium (a full house by this school's standards). At six dollars per ticket, half of the gate was starting to turn into a pretty good budget for the team's next season except for the fact that Coach was not getting any of the money for this particular week.

A few days earlier, the principal called Coach in for a meeting and told him that the Associated Student Body (ASB) was in debt, and that they needed to keep all the money from the gate and concessions from the upcoming game. In return, he was offered all of the gate and concessions for the last home game of the year if he agreed to let the school have that week's proceeds. Coach was ok with this and agreed to allow ASB (which may or may have not been the actual reason, but the one that was given nonetheless) to have the money from Friday's homecoming game.

Coach was fine with this move as attendance—even for regular games—had picked up dramatically on both sides of the aisle since the school was now in a battle for first place. So even though it wasn't the same numbers as the week before, he would still do quite well for the team by keeping the proceeds from the last home game of the season.

Whether or not you are in education, you probably have a good idea of what happened next.

About ten minutes before the last game started, RAD approached him and told him in a jovial manner, "You get nothing, again." No rationale or explanation was given; just that he simply gets nothing. This obviously upset Coach quite a bit. Why is the vice principal in charge of discipline telling him what he can and cannot keep in terms of an agreement that he made with the principal just a few days earlier?

Coach, however, would not let this happen. He walked over

to the two sheriffs on duty (it's fairly common practice to have a few sheriffs on duty for a game) and told them that RAD was literally stealing the money that rightfully belonged to the football program. The sheriffs then stepped in and stopped this from happening. Needless to say that RAD was not very happy, and if he wasn't happy then, more than likely, neither is the superintendent.

The following Monday Coach was called into the principal's office where he [the principal] apologized for what had happened and that the vice principal was out of line. He also went back on his word about letting Coach keep the entire take from Friday's game and told him that he was only going to get to keep half. So to sum up the last two weeks: He received no money from the record setting homecoming game, and only half from the last home game of the year. Needless to say this irked him quite a bit, but there was simply no arguing and Coach was willing to take what was offered.

After the season was over, Coach and RAD had to come to an agreement on some things so that this last second we-are-keeping-all-of-your-money nonsense would come to an end. RAD agreed that coach could keep half of the money for every home game if he also paid for the adjunct people (not including the referees as this was already paid for out of another account) that worked the games such as the announcers, ticket takers, clock operators, and any other people that were involved in running a game. Coach agreed only because this time it was on paper, which meant that he would not have any issues in keeping half for the next football season.

—

In addition to coaching football, he also decided to help out with the basketball program. With the basketball coach turned administrator long gone, and the head coach a former student and baseball player during Coach's years of running the baseball program, he didn't mind taking on the role of the freshman basketball coach in order to help build up the program; as there was at the time no ninth-grade basketball coach to begin with.

During one of the games, a student (coincidentally a freshman football player and also someone who tried out for the freshman basketball team but didn't make the squad) was yelling obscenities at the referees from the bench (even though the student didn't make the team, Coach allowed him to sit with them on the bench) every time a call was made regardless of which side the call actually favored. After a couple of minutes of this as well as ample warnings, Coach told the student that he had to either stop or leave the gym.

Not only did the student not stop with the yelling at the refs, but he would also not leave as Coach asked him to do; which left him in somewhat of a bind as to how to handle the situation.

Now, you might think that the person being paid to do discipline (which is the RAD who told Coach, "You get nothing") for the school would have helped to take care of the situation, but said person—nor any other administrator—was at the game. You might also think that security would help to take care of the situation, but the school has very little security in the afternoon, and Coach also had no way of contacting them.

After nearly a quarter (eight minutes) of this student using profanities towards the referees, Coach realized that he was going to have to do something as the student was just not letting up. Understand that this was not an atypical day for this one particular student. He had a long history of similar behavior towards teachers as well as peers, and had many trips to the counseling and the discipline offices, but was essentially always told to go back to class. In other words, his actions had been tolerated by the schools in the district for many years leading up to this one event. But at a school that tells its students who show up late on a daily basis that are also clearly high as a kite and (instead of calling parents and dealing with the situation as it should be dealt with) are told to "wash up and go to class," (still high by the way), it shouldn't be much of a surprise to anyone that the behavior demonstrated by this student was not only never dealt with, but has come to the point where it [being the behavior] is simply ignored by administration.

Coach then took it one step further and told the student that if he wanted to continue to be on the football squad that he had to stop immediately, or he [being the student] would be removed from the program. This seemed to have done the trick as the student then got up and walked out of the gym sticking his middle finger up at Coach while on the way out.

A few minutes later the student returned to grab his bag that he apparently forgot. At first, Coach didn't let him take the bag because it was next to the players' bags and he [Coach] wasn't sure if it was his [the student] bag he was taking or one that belonged to the players—so he grabbed the student by the arm to stop him (remember this part, as RAD will be using it against Coach). After checking with the players, he realized that the bag did indeed belong to the student and let him take it. The student then began to walk out of the gym again, but not without uttering a few loud obscenities once again towards Coach and anyone else in ear shot.

A few more minutes passed and it was now half-time. The student showed up again, but this time with an older sibling (in his mid twenties) along with two other adults who wanted to start a fight with Coach over what had happened. By now, the head basketball coach had shown up and talked to the three adults and told them that if they really wanted to discuss the situation that it would have to be after the game. They walked away.

The rest of the game went on without a hitch and Coach apologized to the refs and anyone sitting in the stands for the behavior of the student. The local police were called before the game ended in order to make sure that anything that took place afterwards was done in as calm a fashion as possible. Since there was no actual fight and merely an exchange of words, then there was nothing for the police to do and no report of the incident was filed.

—

The next day, Coach was called into the Human Resource (HR) office and put on paid administrative leave until a full investigation about the incident from the game on the previous day could be concluded. Needless to say that he was a little shocked and confused at the move; but not really too surprised being that the RAD in charge of discipline and the new superintendent were good friends from way back, and RAD at this point—after the whole gate and concession fiasco—really did not like Coach at all. As much of a shock as this was at first, it almost really wasn't after he thought it through. Even the new head of HR (maybe a few months into the job, at best) at the time admitted to Coach as to not knowing how to handle the situation and that it could take a while to resolve itself.

And as for the one student that put Coach into this position? Well, once again go back and refer to how this school handles a habitually late, pot-smoking student, and you probably wouldn't be surprised that initially nothing had happened to the student whose actions were responsible for the situation. It wasn't until some parents (thankfully some stepped up and started inquiring about the handling of what happened) began questioning why Coach was on leave and why no action was taken against the student who caused the raucous and put Coach into that predicament to begin with.

Once parents started digging around, RAD realized that he needed to take action, or he might start to look bad (which he already did to just about everyone except for his buddy the superintendent). So he decided that a two-day suspension was the necessary course of action to take against the student.

So what about the in-house investigation? Care to take a guess as to who led that? You got it: the RAD in charge of discipline. The same RAD that tried to take all of the gate money at the last home game after it had been promised to Coach. The same RAD who would send a student that used profanity towards a teacher back to class and tells the teacher to follow the PBIS steps. The same RAD that would complain that his $105k per year salary (not including benefits) was too low for all of the work he was doing.

Needless to say that after interviewing Coach, parents, the student, the refs, and the student's friends, RAD was able to come up with a fair conclusion to the investigation. But he didn't really interview all of those people involved that should have been interviewed. So who then did he interview? The friends of the student involved in the dispute; that's it, no one else. The problem for RAD was that even the friends of the student went on record as saying that Coach did nothing wrong.

Now you might think that after the interviews were done, Coach would be reinstated and put back on the job, but alas, this is the educational system and this was not the case.

Coach would call the HR department weekly and was only able to talk to the secretary who had no answers for him. Never was he able to get through to the person in charge of HR and get a straight answer. He stayed in contact with the local union representative, but even that person was in the dark. In other words, even though there was no evidence that he did anything wrong, Coach was kept out of the loop for nearly three months until the person in charge of HR finally called in him to discuss the findings.

During this three-month span, Coach was given multiple job offers. Someone like him doesn't stay on the market for very long, and once people realized that he was available, the job offers started coming in. And although there were some good offers, he decided to wait and see what was to come about once the probe came to an end (not to mention that his hands were tied in regards to accepting an offer because of the ongoing investigation).

So what were the official findings of the investigation? Nothing. After three months of investigating, there wasn't a shred of evidence that could be used against Coach. He was cleared of all allegations and allowed to go back to the classroom. The one thing that the district did decide is that they [the superintendent and his cronies] no longer felt Coach was right for continuing with that of his namesake. In other words, he was no longer the head coach of the football team and was removed from the program.

—

Once he returned to the classroom and the students found out that he was no longer to be coaching football, a student-lead petition immediately started going around in order to reinstate him as the head of the football program. RAD did not like this and asked Coach to have a meeting with all of the players and to tell them to drop the petition, and that the program will continue without him. Seriously! After all of this, RAD still wanted something from Coach, but it didn't stop there.

At this point, Coach could have easily just told them to take care of the situation that they had created, but this is not the type of person that he is. He agreed to have the meeting with the players and told them to continue to work hard and that the traditions that he had created can still continue without him.

The players didn't buy it.

The principal and RAD then asked for yet another meeting with him a few days later to explain to them what he had done over the years to get the program to succeed. This information would then be passed along so the new head of the football program could continue with what Coach had originally started. Once again, he could have easily told them to sleep in their made bed, but he couldn't bring himself to do so. He always felt that this was about the players and never about himself. After thinking it over for a couple of days, he eventually agreed to tell the two administrators everything in regards to running the program.

Coach also knew (as he had done this for many years) that the likelihood of the players coming back and the program continuing with the same momentum was pretty much zero. The two administrators (both are RADs by the way, but the vice principal was to such a degree that I have only been referring to him as RAD) really believed that the program, players, and winning would continue regardless of who was in charge; an excellent example of the hubris of RAD if there ever was one.

Anyone with some common sense (which is exactly why these two administrators didn't understand this) would understand that a program (as well as a school) is only as good as those who lead it. With Coach gone and the assistants that he brought in no longer welcomed, it did not take long for the program to fall apart. So did the winning continue as the two administrators said it would? Well that depends on how you translate one win in league and pre-season combined, and that one win was the last game of the season. In other words, it took less than one year to destroy all of the work that Coach did in the previous four years to get the program to go from three consecutive winning seasons to a one and eight record.

From another perspective, it took one student with a history of bad behavior, and one RAD who was not fond of Coach from the very beginning, to take down an entire program. What really takes the cake here is that the student, the vice principal, and the principal are no longer on campus.

The student in question transferred to another high school at the end of the year. The RAD in charge of discipline found a higher paying job (after completing the now standard two years at this district) at another district and, to my knowledge, was told half way through his second year at his new, higher paying job that his services were no longer needed at that district. That's right, it took two people that are no longer around less than a month to destroy a program that took four years to build, and have the person that built the program removed.

As far superintendent that brought in the vice principal in charge of discipline, he was released less than one year into a two year extension of his contract that he was given over the previous summer (it's standard practice to make these types of decisions at a July board meeting when there is very little in attendance). And since he was released before his contract was up, the district had to buy him out to the tune of about $230,000.

As a side note, if you've ever wondered why so many school districts are broke, many times it doesn't have to do with actual funding received, but more to do with the fact that much of the funding doesn't always make it to the destinations within the district that will help the schools the most. It is because of decisions like these—such as extending a superintendent's contract by two years and letting him go before the first year of the extension had finished—by the school boards that can help you to better understand why so many school sites within any district are hurting for money (a google search of "school board buys out superintendent" will yield plenty of similar stories).

So what about Coach? As I mentioned earlier, someone of his caliber does not stay on the job market for very long. Even though he will be teaching at the same school (at least for the up-and-coming school year), he recently accepted a head coaching job at, get this, the rival district down the road. Apparently, Coach is good enough to lead a team that has multiple CIF football titles, but not good enough to do so at a school that tells students who show up high from smoking some pot to wash up and go to class (I'm fully aware that I said that already, but I really want to stress that one).

The principal eventually found out indirectly through the grapevine. He did not take it too well and gave Coach his first negative evaluation, well, ever. That's right, in over twenty years of teaching, Coach had never received a negative evaluation, and it just so happened that it was after the principal found out that he took the coaching job at the school down the road. Keep in mind this is also the same principal that thought the football program would run itself with the new coaching staff.

Now maybe you are wondering that perhaps the negative evaluation was justified for some reason. In case you are thinking that, here is about a third of an observation that took place during one class period. Please keep in mind that this is what was given to coach as it was written:

Some students were sitting and some were not. It is good to be consistent. There was no stretching. Maybe have cards of all team members for warm up activity. Maybe have all team members on index cards. Students were able to get the puck and start playing while the teacher still was calling out team members. Equipment basket right near court. Did not see teacher going over rules and regulations with students which is important for this sport since it can be dangerous. Having more games will allow more students participating in activity. Do not stress the looser; you might want to say team a go there and b there. You might want to walk around the games so you are not in the middle of the action and can get hit in the eye. Could have their been some drills to practice dribbling and shooting the ball.

No, you did not just misread that paragraph from a high school principal with multiple degrees, along with—at the very minimum—a teaching and an administrative credential. The use of 'their' in lieu of the correct 'there', the incorrect punctuation, and probably the most important part, the metamorphosis of the activity from hockey to basketball. Perhaps this RAD should have used his own advice that he also included in the observation write-up which was, "*It is good to be consistent*".

By the way, remember when I spoke of what little value, if any, there is in a master's degree in education along with an administrative credential? Well, this written account of one period of PE is an excellent example of the result of those ~~earning~~ sitting through classes to get that degree to become a high-paying revolving door administrator. This error laden write-up is the result of years of education as a student, teacher, and administrator. And in a similar fashion as the vice principal in charge of discipline, this principal no longer works for the district. He will be spending his final few years before retirement at another school district; and though I don't know yet what his exact pay will be, based on looking at the salary schedules, he should be in for a nice 5%–10% increase in pay.

As for Coach, he is continuing to do what he does best. He is happy with his new position and tries to harbor no ill will against those at the district—though the majority of administrators who played a part in the case are now gone, as is the one student—that placed a target on his back; but the real victims here are the student/players that enjoyed having him in charge of the football program. They went from having a great coach that worked with them and brought them to the playoffs for three consecutive years, to a program that is right back where it was before Coach took over.

"But in the end, I wound up right back where I started." – Sam 'Ace' Rothstein (Casino, 1995)

All of those years of time and work nullified by one student and one administrator; both whom are no longer on campus. How's the saying go? Students first... right?

Alice: *Would you tell me, please, which way I ought to go from here?*
The Cheshire Cat: *That depends a good deal on where you want to get to.*
Alice: *I don't much care where.*
The Cheshire Cat: *Then it doesn't much matter which way you go.*

Lewis Carroll (Alice In Wonderland)

What really happened before RAD became an administrator...

For-Profit University

-Tired of teaching?
-Want to get out of the classroom?
-Enjoy relocating every two-to-three years?
-Love attending conferences and staying in $300+/per night suites on the tax-payer dollar?
-Are you good at telling people what to do even though you have no idea what it is they're doing?

Then you are meant for the fast paced life of a Revolving Door Administrator. For just $10k and one year of online courses, you can earn that administrative credential. Upon completion, you will finally command the six-figure salary that you so well deserve and can finally get out of the classroom!

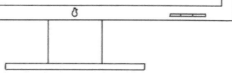

"While the truncheon may be used in lieu of conversation, words will always retain their power. Words offer the means to meaning, and for those who will listen, the enunciation of truth." – V (V for Vendetta, 2005)

Made in the USA
San Bernardino, CA
13 November 2018